# I Used to be Imperfect

### Ian Smith

Copyright © 2023 by Ian Smith

All rights reserved. This book or any portion thereof may not be reproduced, distributed, transmitted, or used in any manner whatsoever, including, photocopying recording, or other electronic or mechanical methods, without the prior, and express written permission of the author or publisher, except for use of brief quotations in a book review, and certain other non-commercial uses permitted by copyright law. For permission requests, write to the publisher at therealdealbooks@gmail.com

Limit of Liability/Disclaimer Warranty: Although the author has used painstaking efforts in making sure that the contents of this book are accurate, it is the reader's responsibility for searching the Bible to make sure that the claims, and contents put forth are correct by not only checking, but verifying.

First printing edition 2023.

All Scriptures references are taken from the King James Version of the Holy Bible in the public domain.

Cover design by Ozzie Angrish-Smith, MBA, MPM
Editor - Ian Smith
Co-editor - Ozzie Angrish-Smith, MBA, MPM

# Contents

| | |
|---|---|
| Preface | V |
| Introduction | VII |
| 1. What is Perfection? | 1 |
| 2. Imperfection and the Reality of Sin | 7 |
| 3. The Result of Imperfection and Sin | 13 |
| 4. The Impossibilities of Perfection-Part I | 27 |
| 5. The Impossibilities of Perfection-Part II | 43 |
| 6. Initial Perfection or Justification | 55 |
| 7. I Used to be Imperfect | 61 |
| 8. The Problem of Justification | 75 |
| 9. The Perfect Example of Perfection-Part I | 85 |
| 10. The Perfect Example of Perfection-Part II | 95 |
| 11. The Perfect Example of Perfection-Part III | 109 |
| 12. The Perfect Example of Perfection-Part IV | 123 |
| 13. Fabricated News | 129 |
| 14. Perfection-Part I | 137 |

| | | |
|---|---|---|
| 15. | Perfection-Part II | 147 |
| 16. | The Possibilities of Perfection-Part I | 159 |
| 17. | The Possibilities of Perfection-Part II | 165 |
| 18. | Ultimate Perfection | 183 |
| 19. | Beyond Ultimate Perfection | 203 |

# Preface

This book is written to bring hope to people who are hopelessly drifting on the ocean of hopelessness. It is also written to provide biblical evidence to support the doctrine of perfection. There are many questions that constantly plague many minds about the perfection question. This has led many to become uneasy and restless. In fact, there are many who have given up in dismay and think that their cases are hopeless.

Many live their lives in constant worry and they fear that, at last, they will lose eternal life and go to hell. They are not at peace with themselves and they are certainly not at peace with God. They appear in public to be happy and their lives seem to be going great, but deep down on the inside of their souls there is turmoil. There seems to be no way out of their lives of worry and fear.

The Bible is the book of God and in it, is found the answers to our deepest longings and questions. Digging deep into this mine of truth leads us to the discovery of the answers to life's most complicated and perplexing questions. The Bible gives us the answer to the many questions surrounding perfection. It is the one book that has been handed down to us at such a tremendous sacrifice. Many have lost their lives, and many were imprisoned for their faith in the Bible. Man has tried to make the Bible extinct, but instead, the very ones who waged war against the Bible have, themselves, become extinct. There is truth in the Bible that if accepted, and practiced, will make one wise unto salvation. It will settle the question as to whether one needs to be perfect.

The Bible tells us that the truth will set us free. The Bible is the truth. Because the Bible is the truth, I want to yoke up with the truth. You will find that when you accept the truth of the Bible that the forces of evil are at your step trying to discourage and turn you away from accepting the Bible as your rule of faith and practice. Satan and his evil host will suggest doubts to you and will try to cause you to lose hope because he knows that if you listen to him and give in to his suggestions, he will get you. The Bible unmasks and exposes the snares that Satan sets for unsuspecting people. He celebrates when he causes a man to fall. There is enough in the Word of God to fly all the traps that the devil has prepared for us.

The reader is encouraged to read and study this book from start to finish. Just selecting any chapter and reading will not give you the full picture. What you want is a solid and complete foundation on which to rest your faith. But if the foundation is weak, you cannot expect your faith to be firm, established, unmovable and unshakeable.

# Introduction

Are you an overcomer and a conqueror or are you a victim and a casualty? Is your life one of fulfillment, peace and joy or are you living out a miserable existence? Are you a reflector of other men's thoughts or are you living by faith in Jesus and enjoying your own personal relationship with Him?

This study of perfection will settle the doubts you may have that have made your life one of worry and will clear up the unanswered questions that you have concerning whether perfection is necessary, and whether it is possible. You will find as your eyes grace the pages of this book, that you will discover many gems of thought that you may or may not have seen or known before. You will realize that it is Satan that tries to obscure the simple truths of God's Word. He shrouds these simple truths in mystery so that we will not discover their beauty, order, and power. He knows that a sincere, and objective study of the Bible will yield wonderful possibilities. One of these possibilities is the perfection of Christian character. He wants to hide this truth because he knows that a discovery of it will take away the worry, doubts, and fears. It will cause transformation of one's life, and that person will be taken from death to life.

There are many distorted versions of how a person obtains salvation and many are confused about the subject of victory over sin. Many have concluded that victory over sin is not possible and so they give up trying to be right in their own eyes, in the eyes of God, and in the eyes of their fellow man. There are many who have given up on trying to be right and so they resort to man-made solutions for their lack of a perfect character.

In studying this book, you will realize that there are some Bible texts that have been misunderstood, and misconstrued by many preachers and Bible teachers. They have used these texts to support their favorite doctrines. They conclude that perfection is not possible and so they pass this false teaching on to their congregations.

There will come a time when there will be a group of people who will so exemplify perfection that God will recognize that fact by sending Jesus the second time to go get them so that they can be part of His heavenly kingdom. This group of ultimately perfect saints will be the "first fruits" or the choicest ones to be presented to the Father and His Son Jesus.

There will also come a time when we will forever be beyond the power of sin. That time is fast approaching. We can see the handwriting on the wall. The events, signs, wonders, disasters, immorality, licentiousness, and prevailing iniquity that is in the world today tell us of the soon return of Jesus to put an end to sin.

Let us wait for the promise of Jesus's soon return. However, we are not to wait in idleness. We are to be actively engaged in warfare against Satan by freeing captives from his prisons. There are many people who have succumbed to the onslaughts of Satan and are held captive in His prisons. They are bound by a life of sin.

They have not discovered the freedom that is found in being free in Jesus.

You will discover that the process of justification and sanctification is designed to uplift man out of the pit in which he has fallen. Through these two processes, man moves from one stage of perfection to the other. Then they ultimately lead him into the gates into heaven and he will live forever.

Our destination is heaven and so we want to make clear paths for our feet. Let us not obstruct the way with man-made theories and teachings on how a man is justified and sanctified, but let us search the Scriptures sincerely and intently to see how we can be saved. The faulty conclusion that many have come to, stating that we are not required to be perfect, has led many millions to their doom and they will find themselves on the side of Satan when the wicked will be arraigned before the bar of God on the charge of high treason.

It is my prayer that as you study this book that you will discover the wonderful truths of perfection, and that you will share the things that you have learned. It is also my sincere prayer that your life will be such an example of perfection that others will see it and be encouraged to want the perfection of character that Jesus has promised to everyone who comes to him in faith, repentance, and contrition.

# Chapter One

# What is Perfection?

As many may or may not know, it is a doctrine of the Bible that anyone who receives eternal life and is given entrance into heaven must be perfect. However, there have been a lot of controversy and debate over whether a person needs to be perfect in order to be saved.

The perfection question has been agitated over and over again and has led to serious divisions among Christians. It is a question that demands answers and one that cannot be ignored. To try and bypass it is to reject the offer of salvation, because it was our Saviour who said **"Be ye therefore perfect, even as your Father which is in heaven is perfect." Matthew 5:48.** This command is coming from Jesus, the Saviour of the world and the Son of God. We have this tremendous declaration about the Saviour that states that "she shall bring forth a son, and thou shalt call his name JESUS: for he shall save his people from their sins." Matthew 1:21. Indeed, it was He who was to save us from our sins; not in our sins.

Before we delve into the overwhelming evidence found in the Bible that show us that perfection and victory over sin are possible, and required, it is necessary to set the foundation that is vital in us understanding and accepting the truth about perfection. We need to define perfection and remove the doubts that have been created as to whether it is necessary. Justice has not been done to the Bible's command to be perfect, and many have the idea that it is not possible, and therefore they resort to some other means of trying to save themselves from going to hell.

Whether one needs to be perfect does not depend on your opinion or my views on the subject. It does not depend on whether I understand it. The Bible is the great standard by which we are to live our lives, and therefore it becomes necessary for us to take a serious look at the subject of victory over sin. This concerns our eternal life and therefore we are under obligation to seek out the truth as it is outlined in the Bible.

We cannot treat this subject casually and expect to find ourselves on the side of Christ when He comes the second time. We cannot allow the comforts of modern living to so blind us to what is required of us to obtain eternal life. In the end it will be seen that to ignore the things that are so necessary for us receiving the gift of eternal life is to be lost. On the other hand, we are to study to find out how to obtain eternal life so we can put ourselves in the position where our hearts are in dead earnest to obtain this gift. When we become earnest in our search for the treasure of eternal life, it moves the arm of God to grant us the desire of our heart to be saved. God cannot save anyone who does not desire eternal life.

There is a lot of worry and confusion among many as to whether perfection is possible. There are untold numbers of people who have given up in dismay, and conclude that it is not possible, and they just go through the motions. They attend church regularly, return tithes, participate in corporate prayer, and look like Christians on the outside. These dismayed souls, practice this "brand of Christianity" by tradition, and are of the group who worry day and night about whether they are saved. They "have no rest day nor night." Revelation 14:11. There is even a class who try to justify their imperfection using the Bible, and in so doing, spread their unbelief to others who are having the same perplexities.

Many would like to be comforted in believing that perfection is not possible and is not required, so they find denominations that preach the "come as you are, and stay as you are" doctrine. They feel justified when they find a body of believers who resort to corrupt versions of salvation to retain their members and to attract new ones. Feeling comfortable is dear to the human heart. It is one of those things that is so subtle that one can mistake comfort for salvation, thinking that, because a minister, priest, or pastor preaches and teaches that perfection is not possible, then he is ok, and there is no need to be all agitated concerning the subject. This person comes to the conclusion that because these teachers of the Bible are professionals, and they went to college or university, they are therefore qualified to be instructors of the Scriptures and whatever they say is true. The Bible has a lot to say about us putting our full trust and confidence in finite man. "Thus saith the LORD; Cursed be the man that trusteth in man, and maketh flesh his arm, and whose heart departeth from the LORD." Jeremiah 17:5.

Are we to look to man to guide us in the right direction? Are we to put our eternal lives into "the men of the cloth?" Does the Bible teach that we are to be so trusting as to put our confidence in ministers, bishops, pastors, and priests? We will see, from a concentrated study of the Scriptures whether this is a wise thing to do. We will so lay out matters as the Bible declares, that no one will be left in doubt as to whether it is safe to put their trust in the teachings of man.

When the perfection question is settled in the mind, it will bring comfort and assurance. The worry and discouragement that once plagued minds will dissipate as a spirit of hope and aspiration takes their place. To be perfect is to have the peace that passes all understanding. To be perfect is to have a heart that does not worry anymore about salvation, but lives in confidence, knowing that your life is hid with Christ in God. To be perfect is to live in harmony with God. To be perfect is to have the assurance of salvation. To be perfect is to have victory over sin. To be perfect is to be freed from the shackles that once bound you to the cart of Satan. To be perfect is to be totally and completely surrendered to Christ. To be perfect is to give up control of our lives and allow the Holy Spirit to be the One who empowers us to repent of our sins and to live lives that are pleasing to God.

Just what is perfection? Let us first look at the dictionary definition. According to Merriam-Webster's dictionary, perfection is "the quality or state of being perfect: such as

a: freedom from fault or defect: flawlessness

b: maturity

c: the quality or state of being saintly"

Many, when they read or hear the word perfection, they immediately come to the conclusion that it, as far as spiritual and eternal things are concerned, means complete sinlessness, but is this so? What does the Bible have to say about this? It is, however, my desire and prayer that as you prayerfully study this book, you will see the truth and that you will have a clearer understanding of this matter of perfection, and know for sure that your calling and election are sure.

God is very clear in telling us that to be willingly ignorant of eternal issues is to invite destruction. He also tells us that to ignore the issues so vital to our eternal salvation is to choose death. "My people are destroyed for lack of knowledge: because thou hast rejected knowledge, I will also reject thee." Hosea 4:6. Here is a plain statement from God stating one of reasons why people are lost. To be willfully ignorant of the Bible is to choose to be lost and to be cast into hell at the end of the world. To reject knowledge is to reject the Source of knowledge, who is Christ, and thereby God rejects the one who does not see his need of obtaining a knowledge of Him. Can anyone obtain eternal life by continually rejecting God? This text is very clear and tells us the reason why people lose eternal life. Let us not stifle our consciences into believing that we can persistently reject the doctrines contained in the Bible and still be permitted into heaven. **"There is a way that seemeth right unto a man, but the end thereof are the ways of death." Proverbs 16:25.** To follow our own inclinations and ideas is to put ourselves on the road to perdition and death. Our own views and opinions are not safe guides and cannot be trusted. Only the source of knowledge, which is the Word of God, can be trusted. All other ways put us into the sinking sands of doom, gloom, destruction, and death.

Just exactly how a person becomes perfect enough to be qualified for receiving eternal life is a question that requires an understanding of the plan of salvation as outlined in the Bible. Many will be surprised to see how God has made the way of salvation plain enough that even children can understand it. The way of salvation is so clearly taught in the Bible that no one needs to stray from the path of righteousness and truth. The beauty and process of salvation is so clearly revealed in the Bible that once a person accepts the offer of salvation, repents of his sins, and is justified, he is perfect. However, do not get too comfortable into thinking that perfection only requires the acceptance of the gift of salvation. We will get into the details concerning the process of perfection as we dig deeper into the mine of truth.

The time has come for us to remove the clouds of doubt and worry that we have been in about this matter of perfection and forever put them to rest, and bask in the assurance of the presence, protection, power, and guidance of the Holy Spirit in us. Many have toiled under a heavy load of guilt for a long time, and long for relief. Isn't it time to shake off the chains that have bound us to the lies and deceptions of the devil? Isn't it time to have victory over sin instead of constant failure? Aren't you tired of being tired? Don't you long to be freed from sin?

# Chapter Two

# Imperfection and the Reality of Sin

Imperfection means "the state of being faulty or incomplete." Google.com. There are many synonyms for imperfection such as "flaw, defect, weakness, fault, deficiency." Google.com.

Just what does the Bible have to say about imperfection? In the context of the subject in question, we must look at imperfection in its relation to sin. In looking at this we must also define what sin is and what are the consequences of continuing in it.

Is there any possibility that man can gain the victory over sin in his own strength? Can our own works of righteousness commend us to God and cause us to be accepted of Him? Just what is it that causes us to be justified in God's sight?

As we dig deep into the riches contained in the Bible, it is my desire and prayer that the doubts you have will be cleared up by getting the correct understanding of what is necessary in order to obtain perfection. For us to get to the bottom of the question as to whether perfection is required of us, it is essential for us to know certain basic things such as why we need perfection, and the vanity and results of imperfection.

## **The Reality**

What is sin? The Bible defines sin as the breaking of the law of God. **"Whosoever committeth sin transgresseth also the law: for sin is the transgression of the law." 1 John 3:4.** This is the correct definition of sin. Once we accept this truth, we can move on in this quest to find out if God is satisfied with imperfection or perfection.

Because there is only one definition of sin and that is "the transgression of the law;" it therefore becomes obligatory on our part to discard man-made definitions. Some say that their very nature is sin itself. This view does not harmonize with the Bible's own definition. If a person is going to define sin as our very nature, then this means that it is not necessary to overcome sin because it is our very makeup. This is a lie from the pit of hell that needs to be slain, buried, and forgotten. To say this, is to oppose God and the Bible. In accepting the Bible's definition of sin and what causes a person to sin, we conclude that a person sins when he makes a choice to disobey the law of God.

Let us look at several Bible texts that talk about sin and our true and natural condition as it relates to sin:

1. Psalm 51:4- "Against thee, thee only, have I sinned, and done this evil in thy sight."

A person might do wrong and sin against another person, but ultimately, all sin is against God.

2. Romans 3:23- "For all have sinned, and come short of the glory of God."

Everyone that has ever lived on this earth has sinned. Of course, we know that this does not include our Lord and Saviour Jesus Christ. This is the reality of sin. However, this does not mean that it is ok to willingly go on sinning.

3. Romans 7:14- "For we know that the law is spiritual: but I am carnal, sold under sin."

We are naturally slaves to sin. We are in bondage to sin. This is our true condition without Jesus in the life. This is no excuse to deliberately continue in sin. Let us not forget that sin is the breaking of the law, not what we are.

4. Rom. 14:23- "For whatsoever is not of faith is sin." The Bible tells us that "the just shall live by faith." Rom. 1:17.

If we are not living by faith in Jesus we are living in sin. It is that simple. It is Satan that has taken the simple truths that are contained in the Word of God and clothe them in mystery. Let us not complicate the Scriptures to our own detriment and death. Our understanding, appreciation, and practice of God's Word are vital if we are to have any hope of surviving in this great conflict between good and evil.

5. Galatians. 3:22- "But the scripture hath concluded all under sin, that the promise by faith of Jesus Christ might be given to them that believe."

We are all naturally under the dominion, captivity, power, enslavement, and imprisonment of sin. This is our natural condition. This is our true state. To deny this is to deny the Bible. To fight against this is to invite the suggestions of demons. So let us humbly receive the truth into our hearts that we might not sin against God. However, this does not mean that our very nature is sin. We are given enough power to overcome and defeat this natural tendency.

6. James 1:14-15- "But every man is tempted, when he is drawn away of his own lust, and enticed. Then when lust hath conceived, it bringeth forth sin."

This text proves, without doubt, that sin results from lusting after temptation. Can the Bible be clearer on this? Sin originates in the mind of man. Lust is unholy desire in this context. When lust is given life where it originates, that is, in the mind of a man, it bringeth forth sin.

7. James 4:17- "Therefore to him that knoweth to do good, and doeth it not, to him it is sin."

If a person knows what is right and does not do what is right, he is sinning. Very plain and straight-forward.

8. 1 John 5:17- "All unrighteousness is sin."

Unrighteousness is wrong doing, evil acts, sinful acts, wrongful acts, and wickedness. The Bible is so plain that we need not get confused when it comes on to the matter of sin.

We can conclude that we naturally desire to sin and break God's law. This is the reality of sin. To recognize our true and natural condition is one step in the process of overcoming sin. If we are to be victorious then we must acknowledge our sinfulness. We are naturally unrighteous, unholy, sinful, rebellious, and selfish. We cannot expect to join in the victory over sin if we deny our natural condition.

Before we get into how to obtain perfection it is necessary that we look at the natural condition of man before and after he sinned in the first place. By establishing this, we can accept the realities and then exercise faith in the possibilities and provisions of perfection.

## Man's Condition Before the Fall

What was it like to live on this earth before sin entered into the world? When God created this world, it was perfect. "And God saw every thing that he had made, and, behold, it was very good." Genesis 1:31. Everything and everyone was perfect. There was no sin and no results of sin anywhere on the earth. God created our first parents and they were perfect. They had no sin in any way. Their intellect was perfect. They had not a trace of disease. They were immortal. They had perfect health. Jesus was personally among them and they walked side by side with Him. There was no barrier between them and the Lord. Angels were their companions. The animals were in subjection to them and man and animal lived in peace and harmony.

Things were going well in the newly created earth until Satan tempted Adam and Eve to sin by disobeying God's commandment not to eat of the fruit of the tree of the knowledge of good and evil. This they did and the floodgates of sin and evil entered the world. Ever since that time, sin has grown to exponential proportions in the earth. Sin originated in the mind of man in the Garden of Eden. A delineation of this is portrayed in Genesis 3.

The sooner that a sinner recognizes his condition of being a slave to sin is the sooner he will be brought to the condition where he can receive and apply the necessary antidote for his slavery to sin. When the sinner sees sin for what it really is, he also sees his utter helplessness in trying to atone for his wrongs. It is therefore imperative that he seeks a solution for his condition from a source outside of and apart from himself. We already read that all have fallen short of the glory of God and sin is the breaking of the law of God, so, if we are to be brought into harmony with God, we must abandon sin. We will get to this tremendous conclusion as we carefully study the truth about the solution to sin and the necessity of perfection.

All willful sin is imperfection and so, in order for a man to become perfect in God's eyes, willful sinning must not be present.

# Chapter Three

# The Result of Imperfection and Sin

We have already established man's natural condition of being a slave to sin. We have concluded that all imperfection as it relates to spiritual things is sin, and so we can now look at the results of it.

When Adam and Eve sinned against God by disobedience to His command, it resulted in them fleeing from God. They even discovered that they were shamefully naked and tried to make clothes that would cover them, but it was not enough. God made them suitable clothing and clothe them. This act of clothing man in suitable clothing, is in itself, a lesson in justification where we are clothe with the robe of Christ's righteousness. One lesson to be learnt from the aftermath of sin is that it leaves us without the garment of Christ's righteousness and we are left with the nakedness of sin.

Just exactly what resulted from sinning against God in the first place?

## 1. Physical Death

Adam and Eve knew of nothing but perfection before they sinned. God had told them that if they ate of the tree of the knowledge of good and evil, they would die.

> "And the LORD God commanded the man, saying, Of every tree of the garden thou mayest freely eat: But of the tree of the knowledge of good and evil, thou shalt not eat of it: for in the day that thou eatest thereof thou shalt surely die." Genesis 2:16-17.

The pair were now subject to physical death because of their disobedience to God. Eve was deceived by Satan into thinking that eating of the forbidden fruit from the tree would not result in death. Was she so wrong! She then became a tempter herself, and Adam chose to sin against God because he did not want to be separated from her. He allowed love for her to dictate to him whether he should obey God.

Adam reasoned that since Eve did not immediately die as a result of her sin in eating the fruit, then it might very well be that he could also eat the fruit and not die. He was willing to brave the consequences and hope that death would not be the result. He reasoned that since she did not immediately die from eating the fruit, then the words of the serpent must be true. Satan, "that Old Serpent," had convinced Eve that she would enter into a new sphere of knowledge, wisdom and understanding, and that she would become godlike. Many today, are so inflated with their own accomplishments that they seem to think that they are so great. They think that they are so wise and intelligent that they do not see their need of God. They trust in their own wisdom and fool themselves that they are their own gods, and that they have to answer to no one, neither God nor man. They become selfish and self-centered. They have rejected the Bible and its teachings and so they have substituted themselves as their own saviour. "Behold, his soul which is lifted up is not upright in him: but the just shall live by his faith." Habakkuk 2:4.

Adam and Eve were barred from eating of the tree of life after they sinned because this was the source of their immortality.

> "And the LORD God said, Behold, the man is become as one of us, to know good and evil: and now, lest he put forth his hand, and take also of the tree of life, and eat, and live for ever: Therefore the LORD God sent him forth from the garden of Eden, to till the ground from whence he was taken. So he drove out the man; and he placed at the east of the garden of Eden Cherubims, and a flaming sword which turned every way, to keep the way of the tree of life." Genesis 3:22-24.

They were driven from the Garden of Eden and eventually died because we read that "all the days that Adam lived were nine hundred and thirty years: and he died." Genesis 5:5. Although Adam sinned, the vitality that God had endowed him with caused him to live for nine hundred and thirty years, along with his temperate lifestyle, the life-giving effects of the tree of life accompanied with his obedience to God and his connection with Him.

Death was the result of the first sin, and death has been the lot of everyone that has ever lived on this planet. It is a reality that is burnished into our brains. We are all subject to death because of sin and we are all mortals because we do not have access to the tree of life that was in the Garden of Eden. This tree is in the New Jerusalem right now because we read about it in the book of Revelation.

> "And I John saw the holy city, new Jerusalem, coming down from God out of heaven, prepared as a bride adorned for her husband. And he carried me away in the spirit to a great and high mountain, and shewed me that great city, the holy Jerusalem, descending out of heaven from God." Rev. 21:2, 10.

> "And he shewed me a pure river of water of lie, clear as crystal, proceeding out of the throne of God and of the Lamb. In the midst of the street of it, and on either side of the river, was there the tree of life, which bare twelve manner of fruits, and yielded her fruit every month: and the leaves of the tree were for the healing of the nations." Revelation 22:1-2.

This is significant. In basic English, there is a clear distinction when something is referred to as "a" versus "the." "The" refers to something specific. This text says that on either side of the river was there "the" tree of life. Aren't you glad for the fact that this same tree of life that was in the garden of Eden is present in the holy city, "the New Jerusalem," and that it will be given to those who are saved from sin and make it to heaven where they will be forever beyond the power of sin? I am so excited that we will one day live forever if we remain faithful to God in this life.

**2. Eternal Death**

If physical death was the end and there was no promise of eternal life for both the righteous dead and the righteous living at the second coming of Christ, along with the judgment of the wicked at the end of the world, then there would be no point in writing this book because we would eventually die and that would be the end of that. However, there is more to this matter of sin than just physical death. The matter of eternal death comes into play. This is a spiritual matter and requires more emphasis than many give it. The subject of eternal death is consequential and cannot be just glossed over.

When God told Adam and Eve that if they ate from the tree of the knowledge of good and evil, they would die, it was not just physical death that He was talking about only. He was telling them that sin would also result in eternal death. That day when they sinned was the day when they became eternally separated from God. If God had not intervened to save man, eternal death and damnation would have been their lot forever. I thank God that we serve a Creator who delights in mercy. However, eternal death comes after the lost face the judgment and are pronounced guilty for acts of rebellion against the government of God. No pen can describe the guilt, horror, shame, and regret which will accompany the wicked when they appear before the judgment seat of Christ for the charge of high treason. It will then be seen that to reject the commandments of God is to die a death from which there is no escape.

When all sin is dealt with at the end of the world, the wicked, who will be burnt up by the fires of hell, will have a sense of extreme guilt and the torture of eternal separation from God. Their end is eternal death. Jesus felt this guilt and torture, and bore it in Himself in the garden of Gethsemane and on the cross. We will deal with the overwhelming and indispensable essentiality of the cross in a later chapter. There is more to sin that just physical death. Have you ever felt the guilt that has accompanied you when you sinned and done something wrong? This is what the wicked will feel when they are arraigned before the bar of God on the account of betrayal and treachery, except that the torture of guilt will be felt way more extremely than how the guilt of sin is felt today.

"For the wages of sin is death; but the gift of God is eternal life through Jesus Christ our Lord." Romans 6:23.

From this text we can clearly see that sin brings forth death as its toll and payment. We also see that the gift that God offers everyone is eternal life if we do not want to reap the eternal death that results from sin.

The Bible tells us that the wicked who are lost will be burnt up by hell fire. There is a spurious and erroneous doctrine that states that man will continue to burn in hell fire eternally, without end. Is this really what the Bible teaches? Can you really conceive of a God who could stand to see man suffering in torture without end? This teaching has driven many to atheism and insanity and this cannot be the character of a God that we are told of in the Bible who is merciful. It is true that the wicked will burn in the fire, but this burning comes to an end.

> "For, behold, the day cometh, that shall burn as an oven; and all the proud, yea, and all that do wickedly, shall be stubble: and the day that cometh shall burn them up, saith the LORD of hosts, that it shall leave them neither root nor branch." Malachi 4:1.

This text clearly states that the wicked will be burnt up. To firmly crush any idea that a soul that loses eternal life will burn without end, we continue to read:

"And ye shall tread down the wicked; for they shall be ashes under the soles of your feet in the day that I shall do this, saith the LORD of hosts." Malachi 4:3.

The wicked are reduced to ashes by hell fire. This text should forever settle any doubts as to whether the wicked will burn forever.

As much as the Bible teaches that the wicked, who are lost, will not burn without end, it must not give anyone the idea that he can continue in sin without consequences. The wicked will be cast into the lake of fire in the end. When sin and sinners, and the devil along with his evil angels are destroyed, a new heaven and a new earth are created.

### 3. Evil Thoughts

"And God saw that the wickedness of man was great in the earth, and that every imagination of the thoughts of his heart was only evil continually." Genesis 6:5.

As the human population of the earth began to increase, the female population also saw growth in numbers. The righteous descendants of Seth saw the women who were from the descendants of Cain and lusted after them because they were beautiful to look upon. They went to them and formed marital unions. This was contrary to the will of God because light and darkness cannot dwell together. The sons of God, as they were called, let their guard down and mingled with these women and eventually married them. This union produced a race of men who were very violent and only thought of evil continually. The Lord saw the wicked condition of the earth and decided that this great wickedness must be destroyed.

> "And it repented the LORD that he had made man on the earth, and it grieved him at his heart. And the LORD said, I will destroy man whom I have created from the face of the earth; both man, and beast, and the creeping thing, and the fowls of the air; for it repenteth me that I have made them." Genesis 6:6-7.

The Lord was sorry to see the low and depraved condition that man had descended into. With all the history and presence of the garden of Eden, the fall of man, and the appeals and entreaties of Adam, men refused to give their hearts and beings to God. They were stubbornly rebellious against the authority of God and chose to live for the temporal things of this life. Their minds were so engrossed with the things of this world that they did not want to make room for the holy things of God to occupy their time, and their thoughts. It seemed more attractive for them to follow their own pernicious ways than to allow God to reign supreme in their hearts. Satan took control of them because they were not decidedly on the side of God.

### 4. Selfishness and Self-centeredness

Because we are naturally selfish and self-centered, it is not in our own power to become kind and caring. We simply do not possess the power in ourselves to become righteous. The natural man is selfish. The Bible states that "the carnal mind is enmity against God: for it is not subject to the law of God, neither indeed can be." Romans 8:7. There are a number of names that can be substituted for the phrase "the carnal mind." Here is a list of them:

1. The natural man
2. Sinful nature
3. The old man
4. The flesh
5. Human nature
6. Corrupt nature
7. The fallen nature

We are not to think that because we inherited Adam's sinful nature that this is our lot so we can go on willfully sinning until Jesus comes. We will examine the possibilities and promise of victory over sin and the command to abandon a life of imperfection and sin for a life of constant victory over sin and the maintenance of the sanctified life.

Man was created in the image of God in the first place, but since Adam sinned against his Maker and opened the flood gates of woe and pain, his descendants and offsprings were naturally selfish. The Bible states that "Adam lived an hundred and thirty years, and begat a son in his own likeness, after his image; and called his name Seth." Gen. 5:3. This is the natural man. When a child comes into the world, he receives the sinful natures of his parents. Note: Sinful nature is not sin. Remember that sin is the transgression of the law.

Selfishness or self-centered love manifests itself in several ways. It is not possible to list all the ways that self-love shows itself, but a short list will give you some idea of the results of this most dangerous of sins in the human heart. They are as follows:

1. Disregard for the welfare of others
2. Looking out for one's own self with no regard for others
3. Egotism
4. Self-pleasing
5. Greed
6. Sinful lust
7. Despotism

We see the results of selfishness manifesting itself daily. The news is so filled with the daily accounts of selfish and wicked acts that it seems as if our senses have become benumbed to these crimes that are daily carried out. Satan is constantly imbuing man with his own character of selfishness that caused his fall in the first place.

Selfishness is naturally cherished in the human heart, and it will naturally seek to display itself at the expense of others. The many wars that have been fought over the centuries, are in a large degree, the result of the spirit of selfishness that pervades the world. Millions of people have lost their lives because of the greed of a few.

We see this ugly character trait of selfishness showing its mean self in the business world. There are constant mergers of mega companies that not just threaten, but wipe out the livelihood of hundreds and even thousands of employees at a time. There are many scams and schemes that men invent to rob others of their money and wealth, and yet we call it business. There are more fitting names for this atrocity that has been unleashed on modern man. The world is so caught up in this theft that the few who manifest a tender regard for the plight of the poor and neglected ones seem powerless to stop the grasping, robbery, and wholesale swindling that is now the order of the day. The struggle for survival has produced a race of people that have become so accustomed to it that very few even care whether their business practices will negatively impact others. We could go on and on about the evil practices of business in the world today, but we can summarize this by simply calling it selfishness.

Paul, in his second letter to Timothy, tells us about what the condition of things would be like in the last days before Jesus comes. The first characteristic of men in these days should be no surprise to us.

> "This know also, that in the last days perilous times shall come. For men shall be lovers of their own selves, covetous, boasters, proud, blasphemers, disobedient to parents, unthankful, unholy." 2 Timothy 3:1-2.

We are indeed living in dangerous times. Paul states that perilous times shall come. They are here. There is overwhelming evidence from the Bible, history, and the state of society that tells us that we are living in the last days of life on earth as we know it. It is hard to ignore this fact. The practice of selfishness is so prevalent in the world that it is the "norm." Being "normal" does not mean right. The standard for right is the Bible. We are not to go by what is popular or even unpopular to determine what is right. A thing may be lawful according to the government or state, but this does not prove that it is righteous. A thing may be unlawful according to society, but may be lawful in the eyes of God. Our first duty is to God. If the laws of the land contradict the Bible, we are to stand on the side of the Bible even if it costs us our lives.

**5. Pride**

Pride is "inordinate self esteem; an unreasonable conceit of one's own superiority in talents, beauty, wealth, rank, or elevation in office which manifest itself in lofty airs, distance, reserve, and often in contempt of others." Noah Webster's Dictionary. Google defines pride as "a feeling of deep pleasure or satisfaction derived from one's own achievements......." We see this everywhere we go. Pride results in strife, competition, fights, and scores of other evil traits.

It was Lucifer, who later became Satan, or the adversary, that invented this evil thing called pride which is sin. **"Thine heart was lifted up because of thy beauty, thou hast corrupted thy wisdom by reason of thy brightness." Ezekiel 28:17.**

Pride originated with him and is a selfish trait of character that has its roots in the sinful nature of man that first manifested itself after Satan convinced man to rebel against God. He had lost his habitation and position in heaven and endeavored to imbue man with the same evil trait of pride.

The practice of competitive sports is a source of pride that is all over the world. The struggle to outdo another causes anger, hatred, and pain. Many have become enemies because of the practice of sports.

Pride is the natural outworking of a power that is entirely opposed to the character of Christ and the law of God. Our first duty is to God, and the first commandment strikes at the door of pride. It tells us that we are not to be so caught up in ourselves so much so, that we place ourselves on the throne of our hearts instead of the meek and lowly Jesus.

"Thou shalt have no other gods before me." Exodus 20:3.

### 6. Lust and Sinful Passion

Another result of man sinning against God in the Garden of Eden is lust. The Bible states that the reason the world is so corrupt is because of the sin of lust. **"Whereby are given unto us exceeding great and precious promises: that by these ye might be partakers of the divine nature, having escaped the corruption that is in the world through lust." 2 Peter 1:4.**

Lust is unholy desire in the context of sin and wrongdoing. This demon of lust is detrimental to the human heart and can so captivate a man that he will ignore reason and sound judgment.

Associated with lust is passion. The feeling of passion must be brought under the control of reason and right judgment. If we allow our feelings and passions to control our wills, the results will be dangerous. We will do things and commit sins that will be abominable in the sight of God and disgusting in the sight of man.

Lust or desire leads to abuse of one's self and shows itself in:

1. Drunkenness
2. Anger and violence
3. Gluttony
4. Indulgence of appetite
5. Fornication
6. Adultery
7. Sexual perversions and illicit practices that are too gross to mention
8. Thrill seeking
9. Envy
10. Jealousy
11. Malice
12. Hatred

All these sins are the result of the unholy desire and passion of the human heart. Since this book is about perfection and victory over sin, we will see how we can overcome these sins. We are not to suppose that because we are naturally sinful as human beings, that we are to remain that way. Lust is one of those evil characteristics that Jesus came to uproot and evict from the human heart.

# Chapter Four

# The Impossibilities of Perfection-Part I

The title of this book is "I Used to be Imperfect" and this chapter might seem like a contradiction to some, but let the Bible speak for itself.

Let us examine the Bible to see what it has to say about whether man's own efforts can bring him perfection. In this chapter we will endeavor to prove from the Bible whether we can accomplish perfection and victory over sin unaided by the presence and power of God.

We have already established the fact that when man sinned, he became alienated from the character of God and his nature turned from being holy, perfect, and righteous to being sinful, unholy, imperfect, and unrighteous. If this is what resulted from the first sin and we inherited sinful nature, what is the result of trying to gain victory over sin by ourselves?

The first instance in Scripture that shows us the impossibility of perfection is what man did in the garden of Eden. When Adam and

Eve sinned, they found out that they were sinfully and shamefully naked and decided to flee from God and try to cover themselves using fig leaves.

> "And the eyes of them both were opened, and they knew that they were naked; and they sewed fig leaves together, and made themselves aprons. Unto Adam also and to his wife did the LORD God make coats of skins, and clothed them." Genesis 3:7, 21.

The fig leaf garments that Adam and Eve made were simply not enough to cover their own nakedness. The Lord intervened and made them coats of skin that were sufficient, not only to cover their nakedness, but also to protect them from the elements. This is a fitting illustration of the utter uselessness and worthlessness of trying to become righteous in the eyes of God on our own.

The inability of man to save himself is demonstrated in the tower that man built to reach a height that would protect him from any future flood similar to the one which had previously destroyed the earth. God had promised that He would not again destroy the world by a flood and sent the rainbow as a token of this promise. We see this token of God's mercy in the sky continually. This promise has not changed. (Satan has taken the symbol of the rainbow and has used it as the the symbol of unnatural sexuality.) Thank God that one day, sin and sinners will be no more, and we will see the rainbow encircling the throne of God. The account of man's daring rebellion against God's promise is recorded in Genesis 11:1-9.

God had commanded man to be fruitful, and multiply. They were to replenish the earth. The command was for man to inhabit the whole earth, not just a small portion. After the flood, rebellious man decided to build a city and a tower so that they did not have to live all over the earth.

> "And they said, Go to, let us build us a city and a tower, whose top may reach unto heaven; and let us make us a name, lest we be scattered abroad upon the face of the whole earth." Genesis 11:4.

This was just one of their objectives in building this tower. Another objective in building the tower was to save themselves from another flood. This was contrary to the promise that God had given and was attempted because man did not trust God to keep him safe. They really did not believe God. The result of their attempt at the first skyscraper was not what they desired because something strange happened that could not be accounted for nor explained.

> "Go to, let us go down, and there confound their language, that they may not understand one another's speech. So the LORD scattered them abroad from thence upon the face of all the earth: and they left off to build the city. Therefore is the name of it called Babel; because the LORD did there confound the language of all the earth: and from thence did the

LORD scatter them abroad upon the face of all the earth." Genesis 11:7-9.

This is where the languages of the earth multiplied. The Lord knew that evil would multiply astronomically if everyone congregated and lived in one place. This is why living in the cities of the world is not the best thing. (Country living is best if children and youth especially, are to have the environment that is best suited for their physical, mental, and spiritual development.)

Man-made efforts are the natural attempt of man to try to save himself. The Bible is filled with many instances where people have tried to save themselves, and how they failed miserably. It may seem like a noble trait of character to keep trying to save one's self. In fact, the devil will encourage us to keep trying because he knows very well that when we keep trying in our own strength, we are attempting an impossibility. The people at the tower trusted in themselves to save themselves. How utterly useless it was to build a skyscraper to escape from another flood. They denied the character, power, and might of God. They fooled themselves into believing that they were safe if the skyscraper was high and strong enough.

The Lord put an end to the foolishness of man's failed attempt of saving himself by his own works at the tower by simply confounding his language. This extraordinary phenomenon could not be accounted for and they could not assign this event to natural causes. Communication was rendered so difficult, that "they left off to build the city." Genesis 11:9. Have you ever tried to communicate in your own tongue with someone who spoke a different language? I wonder how that turned out!

The devil has not ceased to tempt man to invent numerous schemes in trying to attempt to save himself or to become perfect. When these schemes are examined and tested by the Bible it is obvious that they do not work and will never work. These attempts at perfection by man's own methods are a failure from the start. We would save ourselves from numerous ills if we would just follow the simple truths of God's Word. We will see in a future chapter just how simple it is to discover, receive, and accept the way that leads to perfection.

By following the simple instructions of the Bible, you will also reach a point in your Christian journey where you realize that you use to be lost in sin, but you are now living a life of righteousness by the means which the Lord in His great mercy has made available and accessible to us. However, anyone who perfects Christian character does not take pride in his perfection, but is humble and does not brag and seek to exalt himself. He does not go around telling others that he is perfect, but is thankful to God that it is He that perfects him. In fact, the closer we come to Christ is the more we see our true selves.

An example of the impossibility of trying to be perfect and obedient to the commandments of God on our own is found in the record of the Israelites' journey through the wilderness. In Exodus 19, Moses receives instructions from God when he went up to the mountain at Sinai.

"And Moses went up unto God, and the LORD called unto him out of the mountain, saying, Thus shalt thou say to the house of Jacob, and tell the children of Israel; Ye have seen what I did unto the Egyptians, and how I bare you on eagles' wings, and brought you unto myself. Now therefore, if ye will obey my voice indeed, and keep my covenant, then ye shall be a peculiar treasure unto me above all people: for all the earth is mine: And ye shall be unto me a kingdom of priests, and an holy nation. These are the words which thou shalt speak unto the children of Israel. And Moses came and called for the elders of the people, and laid before their faces all these words which the LORD commanded him." Exodus 19:3-7.

The children of Israel, in the wilderness, on hearing the commands and directions that the Lord had given them, rashly declared that "All that the LORD hath spoken we will do. And Moses returned the words of the people unto the LORD." Exodus 19:8. This was their own declaration. It is easy for us to make vows and declare intentions. Our intentions and aspirations may be noble and our goals may be admirable, but are our own efforts enough to cause us to have a right standing before God? Will He be pleased with our best attempts? The Bible gives us the answer to this question so let us continue to search the Scriptures to discover this.

In Exodus 20 we are given "the ten commandments" known as the Decalogue. This is the great standard by which men are judged. There is no other standard, and they tell us our duty to

God, and our duty to our fellowman. To disregard them is to invite disobedience and receive the displeasure of an offended God. To walk in these commandments and obey them is to find peace with God, but is it enough to just try and attempt to keep these ten commandments in our own strength?

The ten commandments were written with the "finger of God" and they were inscribed upon stone to show us the perpetuity, continuity, and endurance of them. Moses also received other precepts and commandments, but these were handwritten. The ten commandments were not written by Moses. This was so important because the principles they contain are forever. He did not leave it up to man to declare it, but did it Himself. This is significant, and any serious and honest Bible student will come to this conclusion. The ten commandments are the mirror which reveals to us our true condition and the state in which we are in without God. They are not suggestions, they are not options, but they are commandments. Do them and live.

> "And all the people saw the thunderings, and the lightnings, and the noise of the trumpet, and the mountain smoking: and when the people saw it, they removed, and stood afar off. And they said unto Moses, Speak thou with us, and we will hear: but let not God speak with us, lest we die. And Moses said unto the people, Fear not: for God is come to prove you, and that his fear may be before your faces, that ye sin not." Exodus 20:18-20.

The awesomeness, power, and majesty of Divinity were shown when God not only wrote the ten commandments, but spoke them. They were to be so riveted in the minds of the people, not only of Israel, but also everyone on the earth as long as the earth remained. The voice of God was so majestic, that the people begged Moses to speak to them instead of God.

Verse 20 tells us that one of the reasons why God came down to give us the ten commandments was so that we may stop sinning. Isn't this one of the main reasons for the plan of salvation? To eradicate and evict sin out of the mind and heart of man is God's intention. This is the plan, and we are to cooperate with God in Him carrying out this plan in our lives. (Another reason for the plan of salvation is to vindicate the character of God.)

To try and bypass the ten commandments is to reject God Himself, because you cannot reject any one of these ten without severing yourself from God. It is the devil that fools and tricks men into believing that they do not need them and that God has abolished them. If that is so, then there was no reason for the Son of God being crucified on a cruel cross. We can go on living as we please without fear of consequences or retribution. However, this is not so.

If the ten commandments were cancelled, then we would be released from our duty to be law abiding citizens. Why would it be necessary to obey the laws of the land? I could steal anything that I want. I could kill at will and kill for pleasure. My jealous heart would not hesitate to take other men's possessions. I could lie about anything, and for any reason with no regard for God or man. I would not be obligated to honor and respect my parents and everyone else. I could even disrespect God and fear no punishment.

If my eyes lusted after another man's wife, I could take her away from him and still feel no guilt because I would be right in my own eyes. I could go on breaking God's Sabbath without any fear and consequences.

A whole book could be written about the world without the ten commandments. What a worse condition would be in the world if the principles contained in the ten commandments were not practiced by men! The laws of the land, to a large degree, are based on the ten commandments. If ministers should teach their congregations that they are released from their obligation to obey the laws of the government, how long would they be allowed to continue preaching in the pulpit? There would be widespread backlash, and their reputation would be held in disrepute. They would quickly realize the error of their teachings in casting aside the laws of the land.

If it is not ok to teach men to disregard the laws of the land, then what about the laws of the God of the universe? Doesn't He have a standard by which to govern His subjects? Isn't He King? How daring it is for a man to declare that God does not have a standard to govern us? He may not say this in words, but to teach that the law is done away with, is to imply this. It would be unthinkable for even parents to run their homes without any standards or laws. The children would become very disobedient and disrespectful. The sad reality of the situation is that we even now see the results of lawlessness in the households in our society. One of the characteristics of children in the last days is disobedience to their parents.

> "This know also, that in the last days perilous times shall come. For men shall be lovers of their own selves, covetous, boasters, proud, blasphemers, disobedient to parents, unthankful, unholy." 2 Timothy 3:1-2.

We are living in an age where children are very rebellious against authority, and to add to this already terrible problem is the teaching that there is no God. To teach that there is no God, is to release men from their duty to God because they are not accountable anymore. If we sow to the wind, we will reap the whirlwind.

After the Israelites received the ten commandments and other laws from God, they again declared that they would do everything that the Lord said.

> "And Moses came and told the people all the words of the LORD, and all the judgments: and all the people answered with one voice, and said, All the words which the LORD hath said will we do. And he took the book of the covenant, and read in the audience of the people: and they said, All that the LORD hath said will we do, and be obedient." Exodus 24:3, 7.

This was now the third time that they declared their intention to obey all the commandments of the Lord. Were they successful in their attempt to do this or did they fail? The answer is found in the same book of Exodus. God had commanded Moses to go up into the mountain, and he spent forty days up there with God.

# THE IMPOSSIBILITIES OF PERFECTION-PART I

The people were getting weary of waiting for him to come back down from the mountain and then the unthinkable happened.

> "And when the people saw that Moses delayed to come down out of the mount, the people gathered themselves together unto Aaron, and said unto him, Up, make us gods, which shall go before us; for as for this Moses, the man that brought us up out of the land of Egypt, we wot not what is become of him. And Aaron said unto them, Break off the golden earrings, which are in the ears of your wives, of your sons, and of your daughters, and bring them unto me. And all the people brake off the golden earrings which were in their ears, and brought them unto Aaron. And he received them at their hand, and fashioned it with a graving tool, after he had made it a molten calf: and they said, These be thy gods, O Israel, which brought thee up out of the land of Egypt. And when Aaron saw it, he built an altar before it; and Aaron made proclamation, and said, To morrow is a feast to the LORD. And they rose up early on the morrow, and offered burnt offerings, and brought peace offerings; and the people sat down to eat and to drink, and rose up to play." Exodus 32:1-6.

Forty days later and the people have committed apostasy and broken God's commandments. They had two times before vowed to obey all of God's commandments and now, they became restless, impatient, and rebellious. How could this be? They had just witnessed the awesomeness, power, and majesty of God, and feared at His presence, and now, they are doing the very thing that they were commanded not to do. How is your connection with God? Have you previously experienced the awesome majesty and power of God in your life and yet you have become disobedient to His commandments? Are you living in sin, and are you breaking His commandments?

When Moses came down from the mountain and saw what was done, the anger of God was kindled in him and "he cast the tables out of his hands, and brake them beneath the mount." Exodus 32:19. He could not believe what he was witnessing. The demonstration of the power and majesty of God, the giving of the ten commandments, and the vows that the people made were not enough to keep them from sinning against God. Any attempt to keep the law of God in our own strength is impossible. Anyone who tries this is attempting something that is unattainable. Commandment keeping is more than just an outward demonstration. This outward demonstration of commandment keeping must be the outworking of an intimate connection with God, or else it becomes legalism.

This chapter is important in showing us the utter impossibility of trying to be perfect on our own and how it only ends in defeat when trying to do right in our own strength. There is no way for us as human beings, to work our way into heaven with our own might and power. We have all been found guilty of sinning against God and there is no way of changing the law that says that the soul that sinneth shall die. Therefore, in order to change this trajectory, something must be done for man which he cannot do for himself.

# THE IMPOSSIBILITIES OF PERFECTION-PART I

We will see from a future chapter what must be done in order to receive salvation.

When the children of Israel settled in the Promised Land, Joshua was their leader and they again covenanted with God. The time was approaching, when he was about to die, and before his death, he gathered the children of Israel and spoke to them the words that he received from the Lord. He then admonished them to serve God.

> "Now therefore fear the LORD, and serve him in sincerity and in truth: and put away the gods which your fathers served on the other side of the flood, and in Egypt; and serve ye the LORD. And if it seem evil unto you to serve the LORD, choose you this day whom ye will serve; whether the gods which your fathers served that were on the other side of the flood, or the gods of the Amorites, in whose land ye dwell: but as for me and my house, we will serve the LORD." Joshua 24:14-15.

Joshua counseled them to choose between the Lord and other gods. Again, they responded by saying: "God forbid that we should forsake the LORD, to serve other gods." Joshua 24:16. They said that they would not forsake and abandon the Lord to serve other gods. Were they right in saying this? If they were, then it is possible, in our own strength to keep from sinning, but the response of Joshua declares to us the impossibility of obeying

God's commandments perfectly and with the right motives in our own strength.

"And Joshua said unto the people, Ye cannot serve the LORD." Joshua 24:19.

This was the response of Joshua when the people made their vow. His words are full of meaning and tell us very vividly the uselessness of man's own effort in his quest to become perfect and gain the victory over sin without the power of God. We must look to another source outside of ourselves in order to receive the power to obey every divine precept. Joshua had learned not to depend upon himself in order to be righteous in God's sight.

We today have "the problem of perfection." Why would it be said that perfection is a problem? It is a problem because many of us do not understand how to go from imperfection of character to perfection. Many have skewed ideas as to how to be accounted and remain righteous in God's eyes. The words of Joshua still echo in Scripture telling us that we cannot in our own strength serve God.

The people heard the words of Joshua, telling them the impossibility of their own efforts to serve God, and again responded to him by saying, "Nay; but we will serve the LORD." Joshua 24:21.

It was spiritual blindness and ignorance that motivated them to respond to Joshua by disagreeing with him about the impossibility of serving God in their own strength. How could he convince the Israelites that it was useless and futile in trying to serve God using their own human power and effort?

What a lesson in the struggle for perfection is in this for us! How can mortal man become just before God? Can my own efforts save me? If my own efforts cannot save me, am I released from my obligation to keep the law of God? How can this dilemma be solved? How can I be saved? If I cannot serve the Lord in my own strength, then what must I do? If I want to know how to obtain perfection, then I must be determined to find out how to, by searching the Scriptures, and when I find this out then I must be dead earnest in following the right way. If we want to receive perfection of character then we are going to have to abandon our own way and walk in the way which the Lord has chosen because **"there is a way that seemeth right unto a man, but the end thereof are the ways of death." Proverbs 16:25.** We cannot depend on our own way of doing things because man's way is the way of death and the Bible tells me that **"the heart is deceitful above all things, and desperately wicked: who can know it?" Jeremiah 17:9.**

With all the evidence in the Bible telling us the impossibility of victory over sin and the utter inability of us in our own strength to acquire perfection, how can anyone teach otherwise? It is Satan that moves men to invent other ways to be saved, because he is the adversary, and his work is to lead men to perdition. The Bible is very adamant in declaring to us that our own works of righteousness are utterly worthless in delivering to us the gift of perfection and holiness in God's sight. We cannot buy our way into eternal life by works.

> "If I justify myself, mine own mouth shall condemn me: if I say, I am perfect, it shall also prove me perverse. Though I were perfect, yet would I not know my soul: I would despise my life. This is one thing,

therefore I said it, He destroyeth the perfect and the wicked." Job 9:20-22.

These words were uttered by Job during his tribulation that he suffered at the hand of Satan, the cruelest of tyrants. Job had an understanding of the worthlessness of man believing and saying that he is perfect. To declare perfection is an admission of imperfection, because, the very declaration of perfection cannot make us perfect in God's eyes, and this self-declared accreditation is one of the most insidious of deadly heresies. This self-declaration of perfection is perversion.

# Chapter Five

# The Impossibilities of Perfection-Part II

"But we are all as an unclean thing, and all our righteousnesses are as filthy rags." Isaiah 64:6. This verse of Scripture is one of the clearest in all the Bible telling us how impossible it is, in our own strength, to become righteous, obtain perfection, and gain the victory over sin. We will not get into a discussion about the exact translation of the phrase "filthy rags," but a declaration of this gives us the idea that our own righteousness in God's eyes is disgusting, distasteful, and detestable. We are never to think that human effort can justify us before God. However, this does not free us up so we can go on sinning.

Many think that the Old Testament does not teach us about the way to salvation and holiness as the New Testament does, but this verse of Scripture stands as convincing evidence to the contrary. It tells us that righteousness is not inherent in us. It tells us that we are, by ourselves, unholy and unrighteous. It reveals to us our true condition and dares us to try and obtain righteousness on our own, if such a thing is possible. In fact, Satan even encourages men to seek for righteousness on their own. He will even lead men to join the church, get baptized, and become "very active for God." He will go as far as to influence men to even become "preachers and teachers of righteousness."

Satan knows very well, the worthlessness of human effort in attaining to perfection, and so, he is the originator of the false doctrine of "righteousness by works," which will get us nowhere. Most of the world's religions teach this invention of man, inspired by the devil. There are billions of people in this world today who are convinced that they can get to heaven or attain to perfection by their own righteousness. This deception leads men to invent practices that supposedly bring satisfaction to their own selves. They get the idea that if they can just be good, it will be enough to become perfect and secure salvation and eternal life. This false idea is the result of man being deceived into thinking that he can attain to righteousness and eternal life on his own. The torture and mental anguish which has resulted from the practice of trying to obtain righteousness and heaven by "good works," is worldwide. Men physically afflict their souls, they do long pilgrimages, they live in seclusion, and they cut themselves off from the tender family ties which God has established to gladden man's life on earth.

The doctrine that man cannot be saved by his own works, however, does not release man from his obligation to obey the ten commandments. "The Preacher" as he declares himself to be, tells us to hear the conclusion of the whole matter. "Fear God, and keep his commandments: for this is the whole duty of man." Ecclesiastes 12:13. If our whole duty is to fear God, and keep his commandments, then, how is it that we are told in Scripture that our own works of righteousness cannot give us perfection and victory? How can we reconcile this? The Bible is its own interpreter and we will see how to attain to the perfection of character. It is a very awesome and beautiful picture that we are given and we all must understand for ourselves how to gain victory over every known sin if we are to inherit eternal life.

To demonstrate the weakness of trying to be right and perfect on our own, we now turn to the New Testament to see what it says about this whole matter of the impossibilities of perfection. The writings of Paul give us a picture of the result of the failure of human effort in trying to attain to perfection and gain the victory over sin.

> "For we know that the law is spiritual: but I am carnal, sold under sin. For that which I do I allow not: for what I would, that do I not; but what I hate, that do I. If then I do that which I would not, I consent unto the law that it is good. Now then it is no more I that do it, but sin that dwelleth in me. For I know that in me (that is, in my flesh,) dwelleth no good thing: for to will is present with me; but how to perform that which is good I find not. For the good that I would I do not: but the evil which I would not, that I do. Now if I do that I would not, it is no more I that do it, but sin that dwelleth in me. I find then a law, that, when I would do good, evil is present with me. For I delight in the law of God after the inward man: But I see another law in my members, warring

against the law of my mind, and bringing me into captivity to the law of sin which is in my members. O wretched man that I am! who shall deliver me from the body of this death?" Romans 7:14-24.

The above quotation is a controverted passage and has led masses to many strange and faulty conclusions. Let us prayerfully examine it to see what the Lord is saying to us. Many have even gone as far as saying that this was the condition of Paul even after his conversion. To say that Paul never got the victory over sin because of what these verses say is to conclude that it is impossible to obtain a perfect character and be victorious over evil. This then leads many into presumption and willful sinning. They think that they can go on sinning throughout their lifetime and still obtain entrance into heaven when Jesus comes. Can any deception be so sneaky and sinister! **(If Satan was cast out of heaven because of his sins, what makes us think that we can enter heaven with our sins?)**

This teaching of entering heaven with sin is an attack on the very center of the gospel. It teaches men that they can break God's commandments. It leads men to think that it's ok to struggle to overcome sin and although they may not overcome it, they will still go to heaven in their sin. What defiance! What a lie from the belly or pit of hades! Many there are, who, in their deceived condition, use Romans 7 to confirm themselves in their sins, not realizing that they are on the road to eternal death and that they are being led by Satan to believe that God will let them into heaven when they presumptuously continue to commit willful sin.

Some time ago, I heard a preacher say something like this: "I ain't what I ought to be, but I am not what I used to be." Do you see the deception in this type of thinking? In other words:

> "I am not perfect, but I am doing better than before. I know the standard of victory over sin is the goal to be reached, but I am not their yet. God sees my efforts, and growth. He is with me, in spite of myself. He sees my situations and struggles, but He makes up for it by covering me with the blood of Jesus. The improvements I have made in my life are an indication that I am saved in Jesus, and that if I should not live another day, God would let me into heaven, even though I am struggling to gain the victory over the sins that I am aware of in my life."

This kind of theology is of the worse kind and reminds me of an illustration of counterfeit victory. It's like a man who says that now that he is a Christian, he robs less banks than before he was a Christian. So, for example, if he used to rob one hundred banks in a year, and he is now down to holding up five banks per year, he is doing pretty good. However, is this victory over sin? Can we call this anything great, and is this how the whole matter of perfection and victory over sin works? All this bank robber did was reduce the number of banks he robbed per year, nothing else. If he was truly victorious, the number of banks he robbed per year would have been zero. God does not deal with partial victory over sin. God is not satisfied with partial service. It is all or nothing. Satan only needs a little dedication to him and he has us in his grasp.

Note: God does not reveal all our sins to us all at once. If He did, we would be overwhelmed. At every stage on this Christian journey, we are perfect through Christ. If we live up to all the light that we know we are perfect in God's eyes because Christ is living out his perfect life in us. We have surrendered, and we have chosen to be obedient children. He recognizes this choice and empowers us to be obedient.

Back to what Paul is saying in Romans 7. Verse 14 says "For we know that the law is spiritual: but I am carnal, sold under sin." It must be noted that he is speaking on behalf of all human beings. The natural man is fallen and is a slave to sin. Man is naturally inclined to sin against God. The carnal or sinful nature of man is slavery. Our natural condition is sinful. There is no hope for the carnal nature. Notice I did not say there is no hope for man. If all we could hope for is to remain in our carnal nature, and not have victory over sin, it would then be pointless discussing the subject of perfection. If we have no hope then we are very miserable.

Romans 7:15- "For that which I do I allow not: for what I would, that do I not; but what I hate, that do I." This verse is saying that the very sin which I know is wrong I do anyway, and although I hate to do it, I still do it in spite of the fact that I know it is wrong. I naturally do wrong even when I know it is breaking the commandments. In other words, I willfully sin in the face of my desire not to. My own lust after sin overpowers me although I know it is wrong. This sort of life is dear to the human heart where it has its origin.

Let us constantly keep in mind that this passage of Scripture is talking about man in his sinful nature unaided by God. It is utterly impossible for us to be victorious over sin without the intervention and help of God. This is the only logical conclusion. Many would like to have "a bed of roses" journey to heaven without the sacrifice of sin. They make Romans 7 their defense in living a life of sin and declare that it is impossible to gain the victory over sin, but is this so? Can we come to such an erroneous conclusion with all the evidence in the Bible telling us that no sin will enter heaven?

The Bible does not say that when Jesus comes the second time that men's lives will suddenly be transformed from a life of sin to a life of holiness. However, it does state that in whatever spiritual condition we are in when Jesus comes, is the condition that we will remain in.

> "He that is unjust, let him be unjust still: and he which is filthy, let him be filthy still: and he that is righteous, let him be righteous still: and he that is holy, let him be holy still. And, behold, I come quickly; and my reward is with me, to give every man according as his work shall be." Revelation 22:11-12.

Take note that the declaration to be unjust and righteous still is associated with the second coming of Christ. Verse 12 even goes as far as saying that a man will be rewarded according to his works. In other words, whatever you sow you will reap. The works are either righteousness or unrighteousness. It is either God who worked the works of righteousness in us or we lived contrary to the will of God.

The righteous are saved, but the unholy are lost and die an eternal death.

Romans 7:16- "If then I do that which I would not, I consent unto the law that it is good." This text is simply stating that if I do the very thing that I don't want to do I am agreeing that the law is indeed holy. The very things I do not want to do are the things I know that God's commandments condemn. Therefore, I agree with the righteousness of the law and declare that sin is bad and the law is good.

Romans 7:17- "Now then it is no more I that do it, but sin that dwelleth in me." What is this verse telling us? It is telling us that I sin because of my sinful nature that resides in me. (Sinful nature is not sin because sin is an act, not our nature.) I myself desire to do right, but my carnal or fleshly nature does otherwise if I am not under the control of the Holy Spirit.

Romans 7:18- "For I know that in me (that is, in my flesh,) dwelleth no good thing: for to will is present with me; but how to perform that which is good I find not." This is one of those texts that tells us convincingly that we cannot, in our own strength, do good. My sinful nature that is in me has not an ounce of good. It is good for nothing because it is entirely opposed to righteousness. It is the way of death. I am naturally inclined to do wrong. My whole nature is sinful. Is there any solution to this problem of my sinful nature which is diametrically opposed to holiness?

I want to do right but I do not find any way of doing it on my own. My fleshly nature does not allow me to do good. It fights against my will to do right. This condition is the very nature of what society today, call addictions. It should essentially be called sin. If one allows the clamors of his own lustful and fleshly desires to overpower his will to do right, he becomes an addict, or rightly called a sinner. **We cannot allow ourselves to decorate sin with beautiful colors. We are to call sin for what it really is. Sin is dreadful, earthly, devilish, sinister, abominable, and destructive. It will overpower you if you allow it to take root in your heart.**

It is impossible for us to find anything good in ourselves to overcome sin. This is a tremendous conclusion for Paul to have arrived at. Is the text saying that it is impossible to find the solution for victory over sin in mine own self? Indeed it is. That is why this chapter is fittingly dealing with, "The Impossibilities of Perfection and Victory over Sin." It is impossible to find anything that originates with me to gain the power to overcome all sin. The source of the power is elsewhere.

Romans 7:19- "For the good that I would I do not: but the evil which I would not, that I do." I want to do right but I do wrong. I know what is right but I do not do it, but instead, do the exact opposite. The Lord is here telling us the truth that we cannot look into ourselves to do what is right, because we are going to fail every time we attempt to do so on our own because the motive is wrong, and we do not have the ability to do right to satisfy the claims of His holy law. Can we see the pointlessness and futility of listening to our heart, of following our heart, or obeying our instincts? It is not dependable but will enslave and ensnare us.

Romans 7;20- "Now if I do that I would not, it is no more I that do it, but sin that dwelleth in me." We have repeated for us, the fact that it is the sinful nature that cause us to do the things that we know to be wrong.

Romans 7:21- "I find then a law, that, when I would do good, evil is present with me." The principle of my sinful nature opposing the good that I want to do, is found in me. My sinful nature is in me. If the sinful nature in me is allowed to thrive, it will overpower the good I want to do.

Romans 7:22- "For I delight in the law of God after the inward man." The "inward man" is that part of our nature that is the higher nature and has the ability to receive the holy character of God. This higher power or nature that is in our mind takes pleasure in obedience to the law of God.

Romans 7:23- "But I see another law in my members, warring against the law of my mind, and bringing me into captivity to the law of sin which is in my members." The reason why I go against my desire to do right is that my sinful nature wars against my will to do right. Romans 8:7 goes as far as saying that "the carnal mind is enmity against God: for it is not subject to the law of God, neither indeed can be." My sinful nature hates God and refuses to come under the rule of the law of God. It is rebellious, hostile, and antagonistic against law and order. It always desires to be lawless, and licentious. The conflict between my sinful nature and my will to do right is compared to war. In a typical war, one side wins and the other side loses.

Romans 7:24- "O wretched man that I am! who shall deliver me from the body of this death?" We have now come to a verse of Scripture that is begging help for the desperate condition that man naturally finds himself in without the aid of the power of God. Man cries out in utter helplessness and asks the question, "who shall deliver me?" Man now concludes that it is impossible for him to gain the victory over his sinful nature without the aid of an outside power. He takes an honest look at himself. He does not stubbornly say that it is impossible to gain the victory over sin, but he cries out for help to gain the victory.

There are untold millions of people worldwide who are bound by lives filled with sin, iniquity, lawlessness, and evil beyond belief. They are bound by a force that is stronger than their will to do right. They make resolutions, vows, prayers, and are determined. They cry, they mourn, they try all kinds of self-help programs and yet these are powerless to free them from the chains that bind them to their lives of sin, and wickedness. Every time they believe they are about to be let loose from their chains, they digress. They are in the world without any apparent help. They are indeed saying, "O, wretched man that I am, is anyone able to deliver me from my sinful and wicked life? I am addicted to sinful acts and deeds. Am I ever going to be released from my evil habits?"

The facts concerning the utter desperate nature of fallen man speak loudly and declare that in his own strength, there is no hope for him. By himself, the man of sin in him will forever hold the supremacy without help from another. The fleshly nature of sin cannot be reformed, transformed, or improved. It must be killed. What can be done to the evil tongue? Can the mind eventually think only pure thoughts? Can the passions and appetites come under the control of reason and sound judgment? Can the lower passions be subject to the higher powers of the mind?

There is absolutely nothing that man, in his own strength can do to kill the carnal man. If there is any hope of burying it, then something miraculous must take place. It will be shown from Scripture that the only solution to the problem of "the Old Man of Sin" is for it to be crucified, killed, and buried. The important thing for us to conclude this chapter with is that perfection and victory over sin is utterly impossible and unattainable by man's own effort only. We will examine how this miraculous transformation from the captivity of "the old man of sin" to "the spiritual man of righteousness" is brought about in the life of helpless and abandoned man.

# Chapter Six

# Initial Perfection or Justification

It is a fact that perfection is required for the children of God to enter in through the gates into the New Jerusalem. It is a prerequisite for eternal life. The different stages of perfection must be understood so that we can make intelligent decisions. The way must be correctly and clearly outlined so that a person can make a choice as to whether he wants to travel this road called perfection.

The first stage of perfection is "the initial stage." We can also refer to it as "perfection 101." It may be called the basic stage in that it is the first part of the journey of growth in perfection. This kind of perfection gives us our title to heaven. We can also refer to this initial perfection as justification.

There are millions upon millions of Christians who have distorted views of just what justification is and are just a little bit more knowledgeable of it than the man in the world who cares nothing about His standing before God. Many have heard sermons and read books that speak of justification or initial perfection as it may be referred to. The sad thing about it is that most people have been focused on the wrong thing.

Just what is justification? A very basic definition is that it is simply forgiveness or pardon. It is the act of God the Father in pardoning the sinner and then accepting him just as if he has never sinned.

In examining this first aspect of perfection or justification it is necessary to look at the reason why I need justification. Without this vital ingredient of salvation, I am doomed to death and there can be no hope of ever being saved from sin. My whole life is one of hopelessness and worthlessness if God the Father did not provide a means by which the penalty for my sins could be paid. The reason why I need justification is that I cannot pay the penalty for my sins and save myself. I deserve only death.

**"For the wages of sin is death; but the gift of God is eternal life through Jesus Christ our Lord." Romans 6:23.**

**"Behold, all souls are mine; as the soul of the father, so also the soul of the son is mine: the soul that sinneth, it shall die." Ezekiel 18:4.**

At its very basic level, the reason why we need to be forgiven is the fact that **"all have sinned, and come short of the glory of God." Romans 3:23.** We read that the wages of sin is death. This is what every human being, (except Christ), that has ever lived on this earth justly deserves. Sin is the breaking of the law of God. The only Person that could ever claim that He had never ever sinned was Jesus. Everyone else stands condemned before God. There is nothing we can do to change the record of sin against God. It is what it is. The law pronounces us guilty of death. We have all committed a crime against the government of God and we stand condemned. There are no works of righteousness that we can do that can erase this record. We are powerless to come up with a plan that will reverse our conviction and condemnation, and therefore, as it stands, there is no hope that can be manufactured, developed, invented, carried out, or depended upon that will satisfy the just wrath of God against sin.

Man is powerless to change the record of sin. Let us bring this fact closer home. What If you have robbed fifty banks in the past, can you do anything to change that fact? Of course not. So it is with our standing before God.

If I am going to have any hope of clearing my standing as a law breaker or sinner before the judgment seat of God, then I cannot look to myself. I cannot atone or make up for my sins by working hard to change the record. I stand condemned. My own good deeds cannot change my record. If I sacrifice to help the poor, I am working in vain to deliver myself from what I deserve. If I climb the highest mountain, it will not be enough to change my standing. If I fast and pray till I am pale or blue in the face, even this will not be sufficient. If I faithfully return my tithe every week to the storehouse, it will not plead my cause. If I beat myself in an attempt to change my standing as a sinner in the record books of of heaven, I will still be accounted worthy of death. If I do good works and live a good life, it will not cause me to be forgiven.

Something else must be done for the sinner to be justified. The sinner cannot use his good deeds to make his appeal for pardon. The very fact that we have all sinned condemns us to eternal death only. This is the only way to look at it.

Just what is eternal death? Man was initially created perfect in every way. There was no trace of sin in him. Adam and Eve had no inclination to sin. They were righteous and perfectly holy in the presence of the Lord. They knew nothing of sin until one day they chose to break God's law and severed their connection with God. They tried to flee away from their Maker but He caught up with them and when He asked who told them that they were naked and if they had eaten the forbidden fruit, they began to cast blame on Him and the serpent. The Lord felt the separation sin had brought between Himself and man and that is why He had cried out to Adam saying "where art thou?" Not only did the Lord feel the void in His heart, but they too felt guilt for the first time. The only thing that they deserved was eternal death or eternal separation from their God by being slain by hell fire. This was their just reward according to justice, but God intervened to save them from their sins. We can then conclude that eternal death is eternal separation from God by being destroyed by the fires of hell. At the end of the world, when the city of the New Jerusalem comes down from God out of heaven, the unrepentant wicked will be eternally banished by means of this fire. They will be burnt up and reduced to ashes. This death will seal the fate of doomed sinners. The Bible calls the destruction of the wicked by hell fire "the second death."

Many think that they are unaccountable for the deeds of their lives and they must answer to no one. They have rejected the offer of salvation and are fooled into thinking that when they die, they do not have to face any consequences.

First things first. We are all subjects of the Creator of the earth and the rest of the universe. This makes us subject to His law. If we break it, and we have, we are subject to death. This is the reason why we need forgiveness. This pardon that we all need is the solution to our lost condition. Without pardon the sinner must receive the full and just wrath of God against sin. He must stand before the bar of God on account of high treason. There is no escape. He cannot avoid the court date. Whether or not he wants to show up is not an option. One way or another he will stand in condemnation before "the Judge of all the Earth." "How shall we stand in that great day when every thought and word and action, God, the righteous Judge shall weigh?" F.E. Belden. It is a sobering thought to know the fact that the unrepentant sinner who loses eternal life will stand trembling before the Lord at the end of the world when sin and sinners are destroyed.

Initial perfection is the gift of God. We do not deserve it. We did not earn it. We did nothing to receive it. When we are forgiven of all our sins God looks on us as if we had never sinned once in our lives. This is initial perfection or justification. We are declared righteous. This declaration is not all there is to the plan of salvation because if all that happens to us is that God declares us righteous, then this is one-sided. We are looked upon as being righteous because of forgiveness, but this does not free us to commit sin. This declaration happens when a person accepts pardon from God. The moment pardon is accepted is the moment the sinner is declared perfect. There are untold thousands, yea, millions, who have stopped at initial perfection and think that this is all that is required of God. They think that because they believe that they have been pardoned they are released from obedience to God's commandments and they can go on sinning. The fact that a person is forgiven demonstrates the fact that they have repented from their sins. There can be no initial perfection, no justification, no pardon, no declaration, and no changing of man's standing before God if he has not turned away from his sins.

**Note:** Repentance from sin is the gift of God to us and the willing heart receives this. There can be no repentance from sin if the power of the Holy Spirit has not empowered the sinner to separate from his sins. If we have a sincere desire to seek the Lord, He will be found and if we believe that what He has promised He will do, then He will give us the gift of repentance. This gift of repentance miraculously causes us to turn away from and forsake our sins. Repentance or being sorry for sinning against God and a turning away from it is not inherent in us. It is God, through the Holy Spirit, that leads us to repentance, and we must be ready and willing to receive this gift.

Justification changes our standing before God and He looks on us just as if we have never sinned because we have come to Him in contrition, repentance, confession, and the mindset has changed from one of sinning against God to one of obedience to God. The attitude has been changed and we are no more rebels against God's laws and commandments, but we are subject to them. This initial perfection happens with the consent of the repentant sinner. If we choose to go on sinning, then God cannot declare us forgiven and justified.

I thank God that He has made a way for me to be declared righteous. I accept God's pardon and I turn away from my sins in deep contrition. I am not worthy of the least of God's mercies, but I accept them. I thank God that He looks on me as if I am perfect because I have accepted His gift of pardon, and I have denounced my sinful ways. To God be the glory.

# Chapter Seven

# I Used to be Imperfect

Where do we reach the point where we used to be perfect? The answer is found in the justification that is freely offered to us. God looks on us as though we have never sinned once in our whole life. **THE REPENTANT SINNER DOES NOT SAY "I USED TO BE PERFECT." IT IS GOD WHO DECLARES HIM PERFECT.** Let us explore the ins and outs of this vital subject to see how we are declared perfect by God. How is this initial perfection or justification accomplished? How do I receive justification? By what means is my justification secured? These are questions that are vital and must be dealt with so that we can see how much God loves us and desires to save us. In answering these questions, we will find out just how much has been done to provide for us a means of escaping the wrath to come.

In this stage of perfection, there is and can be no thread of human invention. Justification is not inherent in us as human beings. We have already concluded that doing good cannot justify us or make us perfect in God's eyes. (This does not free us from obedience to the law of God.)

There is only one means by which we are justified and accounted perfect and righteous in the presence of God. This means of justification is the single most important thing that was ever done to declare us perfect and justified. Without this means of perfection and justification, we are eternally lost and doomed.

Let us establish certain things: the law is necessary for me to observe, but law keeping is not the source of justification. Keeping the law cannot save me from the penalty of sin, but it is necessary to keep the law to prepare me for entrance into heaven. Note: It is through the power of the Holy Spirit in me that I am empowered to obey the law.

The necessity and purpose of the law of God is outlined in Paul's letter to the Romans. "By the deeds of the law there shall no flesh be justified in his sight: for **by the law is the knowledge of sin."** Romans 3:20. The purpose of the law is to show us our sins so that we can repent and turn away from them. Sin is very repulsive. **God's will and plan for our lives is that we abandon sin and trade it in for righteousness.** Many people have used the book of Romans to say that the law is not necessary and man is released from his obligation to obey it. Undoubtedly, it has been used to justify their release from the requirements of obedience to the law of God. All that Paul is saying from the above text is that our acts of obedience to the law of God is not what causes our justification. To further prove that the law is binding upon man, we cite Rom. 3:31: **"Do we then make void the law through faith? God forbid: yea, we establish the law."**

Let us think this through. We cannot do anything good or righteous to save ourselves from the penalty of sin, but obedience to God's law is required of us. We must never think that law keeping can bring us justification or forgiveness, but we should never ever think that we are released from keeping the law.

What is the purpose of the law? The whole reason for the law is to reveal our true condition, and point out sin in our lives. The second part of Romans 3:20 states that it is through the law that we become aware of sin in our lives. The law simply exposes sin. Let us remember that sin is "the transgression of the law." The law is there to show us our sins so that we can repent and turn away from them. **If Jesus died on the cross because of our sins, then it means that sin is very offensive in God's eyes. God's will and plan for our lives is that we abandon sin and trade it in for righteousness.** The law cannot save us from the condemnation of sin, but it is to be kept if we would be fitted for heaven. It is the great standard by which man is judged. The laws of governments, whether local or national, are what citizens are judged by. So it is with the government of God: we are judged by His law.

If man did not sin, there would have been no reason for the Lord to have spoken and written the ten commandments, because it was already written in his heart, but, by reason of sin, we needed to have this great standard spoken and written to reveal to us our true condition as sinners.

Because all have sinned, then all naturally deserve death. The law says that the soul that sins shall die. God told Adam and Eve that if they ate from the tree of knowledge of good and evil, they would die. Eventually, they disobeyed God and the judgment of death was pronounced against them. This condemnation must be carried out in justly dealing with sin. We cannot change this fact, we cannot get around it, and we are powerless to stop it. However, a plan was devised by the Father, Son, and Holy Spirit to deal with this terrible emergency called sin. God's law says that the penalty of sin must be paid. The reason why we are offered forgiveness and receive it is simply the fact that the penalty has been paid. It is Satan's plan to deceive us into thinking that because the penalty has been paid, then it releases us from obedience to the commandments of God and there is no need for victory over sin.

Sin cannot live in the presence of a holy God, so if I am to be permitted into heaven, it is expected and required that sin is eliminated from my life. We will deal with this vital stage of perfection called sanctification in a later chapter.

The source and cause of **initial perfection or justification** is not inherent in us. It is elsewhere. What must I do to receive justification or pardon? Can I do anything to receive pardon? Is there anything that can be done for me to avoid the sentence of death for my sins?

In this matter of justification, my role is to simply accept God's offer of forgiveness or pardon that is freely offered by means of His only begotten Son and our Saviour, Jesus Christ. How do I reach the point where I am declared righteous? There are certain things that must occur before I can be declared righteous, perfect, and justified. I must:

1. Behold the love and mercy of God. I must come to the realization that a way has been made so that I do not have to receive the righteous wrath of God against my sins. I must see the love and mercy of God towards me. I must see that I have offended the God of the universe by my sins.

2. I must see my need of a Saviour.

3. Confess and repent of my sins. I can only repent through the gift of repentance. True repentance comes from God.

4. Believe on the Lord Jesus Christ.

5. Believe that the death of Jesus made atonement for my sins.

Let us examine the Scriptures to see the way that is outlined to avoid the death penalty for sin that we all deserve. What must I do to be saved or justified? There are several texts that can be used to answer this question. We will for now deal with the means by which the first stage of salvation which is justification or forgiveness is accomplished. This first stage of perfection is initial perfection or justification.

Justification is received by faith. To show that it is only received by faith we will look at Acts 16:30-31. It reads, "What must I do to be saved? And they said, Believe on the Lord Jesus Christ, and thou shalt be saved." There we have it. We must believe on Christ. He is our means of salvation. Christ is the source of justification. Jesus means Saviour from sin. Christ means the Messiah or the One sent. God the Father sent Jesus on a mission to save us. Believing is accepting, trusting, putting confidence in, and depending on Jesus. Believing in Jesus is not just an assent of the mind to the acceptance of the Source of salvation, but it is also a yielding of the power of the will and affections with a humble reliance on Him for salvation and justification. This justification was not provided by man, and it cannot be developed by man. That is why man is not the source of it. If it were, then we would not need a Saviour. We could, by means of good works save ourselves, but this is impossible, because the just reward of our sins is only eternal death.

In believing on the Lord Jesus Christ, several things are accomplished. They are as follows:

1. We, by faith accept the death of Jesus as atonement for our sins.

2. We are delivered from the penalty of sin which is eternal death.

3. We give Christ the permission to become our Advocate or Intercessor in the court of heaven.

4. Christ accepts our request for forgiveness and presents this before the Father.

5. God the Father is petitioned by Christ on our behalf.

6. The Father does not bypass us because of our condition, but hears our petition because Christ presents us to Him.

7. When Christ petitions the Father on our behalf the only thing that He looks for in us and sees is the character of His Son Jesus.

8. Christ lays our glory in the dust.

9. Christ does for us that which we cannot do for ourselves, and that is to free ourselves from the penalty of sin.

10. Christ presents His perfect and eternal righteousness as our defense.

11. When the Father sees the character of Jesus in us, He immediately forgives and justifies us and we are accepted because of Jesus.

12. We are declared righteous. This is the judicial act of salvation. This is imputed righteousness.

13. We are justified on condition of our future obedience to God's law. We are given an A+ even before we move on to the next stage of perfection called sanctification. (In justification we are declared righteous. In sanctification we are made righteous.)

14. God looks on us just as if we had never sinned once in our lifetime.

15. We are now fitted to move on to the next stage of perfection which is sanctification. (We will deal with this in another chapter.)

All I can say is "thanks be unto God for his unspeakable gift." 2 Cor. 9:15. What a tremendous transaction! How can God erase the sinful record of my past and give me a perfect record of righteousness and holiness? It is far beyond our comprehension. We do not, and cannot fully understand it, but we can accept it. This record of perfection is freely given to us. If we accept it, we are pronounced holy and Christ is holy. This record is initial perfection or justification. The sinner is declared perfectly righteous. We are justified because Jesus obtained the right to be our Mediator by His life, death, burial, and resurrection. Only Jesus was able to accomplish the a task of living a perfectly holy and sinless life while He lived on earth. Here what He says of Himself: "The prince of this world cometh, and hath nothing in me." John 14:30. There was nothing in Christ, the God-Man, that responded to the temptations of Satan. Not even by a thought did Christ sin at all. I am so thankful to God that Christ did not permit His human nature to get the better of Him. He did not allow temptation to overpower His connection with the Father. You too can have that kind of connection that causes you to be invincible against the assaults of Satan because it will be "God which worketh in you both to will and to do of his good pleasure." Philippians 2:13.

Another text that tells us the means of bringing us salvation is found in Ephesians 2:8. It says, "For by grace are ye saved through faith; and that not of yourselves: it is the gift of God." Salvation is a gift from God. This is the reason why justification has in it, not one thread of human devising. In this text and context, grace simply means the unmerited mercy, favor, and compassion of God the Father towards us. Grace allows the perfect and righteous character of Christ to be credited to us. When God looks on us, He does not see our own righteousness, but He sees the righteousness of Christ's holy character in us. This is what is freely offered to cover our sins. The only way for the Father to see the righteous character of Christ in us is for us to believe and accept the gift of salvation with repentance and contrition. There can be no mistake about the means of justification. This is one of the most clearly laid out doctrines in the Bible.

The means by which we are saved is grace (the favor, kindness, and goodness of God towards us), and this grace is a reality in us through the exercise of faith, which is trusting and believing. Through this act of faith, we are delivered from the power and penalty of sin. Grace through faith is the means of receiving salvation and this immediately results in justification. There is no other way of receiving salvation. To stumble over this simple math is to be subjected to the death penalty for sin. The process by which a sinner moves from death to life is not like a long, drawn-out court case. Salvation is received as in a moment. The very moment in which the sinner exercises faith in and accepts the death of Jesus as the atonement and payment for his sin is the moment that he moves from the condemnation of death to the realm of the assurance of eternal life. He repents of his sinful life by the gift of repentance which is given to him and confesses all his sins and he is declared perfect and justified.

The provisions that are made available through the grace of God are astounding and beyond our finite imagination. We are to take advantage of these gracious provisions and rest in the light of the righteousness of Christ.

Since salvation is a gift, and we did not earn it, then we are to simply accept and receive it. Salvation is the ultimate gift. There is no other gift that is greater than the gift of salvation. To be delivered from the penalty and power of sin is the best thing that can ever happen to the sinner. Paul makes it clear that salvation is "not of works, lest any man should boast." Ephesians 2:9. The Lord has made the way of coming to Him so clear that no one need stumble. Have you ever filled out an application? It can sometimes be a difficult task. Just ask anyone who has applied for a U.S. visa or citizenship. But not so with God. The process is made simple through the exercise of faith.

To provide more evidence on the means by which we obtain justification or initial perfection, we now turn to Romans 1:16-17. It says, "For I am not ashamed of the gospel of Christ: for it is the power of God unto salvation to every one that believeth; to the Jew first, and also to the Greek. For therein is the righteousness of God revealed from faith to faith: as it is written, The just shall live by faith."

The gospel or good news is that it is through the perfect and righteous life, death, burial, and resurrection of Christ that we have salvation. In fact, "Neither is there salvation in any other: for there is none other name under heaven given among men, whereby we must be saved." Acts 4:12. There is no other source of salvation, and there can be no other cause of salvation. It is not found in Islam, Buddhism, or Hinduism. We have heard a joyful sound, and it is that Jesus "is able also to save them to the uttermost that come unto God by him, seeing he ever liveth to make intercession for them." Hebrews 7:25. Jesus will pick us up and transform our lives as in a moment, if we only believe in Him and accept the offer of justification He freely gives to us, and repent.

Paul could say that he was not ashamed of the gospel of Jesus. The sinner that has been saved from sin does not seek to hide the gospel, because he welcomes this good news and is joyful in it. He searches out ways in which to share it, and is not afraid to make it known to others. The impact of the gospel on his life is naturally seen because it has wrought salvation in him and it naturally brings the gifts of righteousness, peace, joy, love, and compassion.

The above text says that "the just shall live by faith." We obtain eternal life by faith. We live out eternal life by faith. "But without faith it is impossible to please him: for he that cometh to God must believe that he is, and that he is a rewarder of them that diligently seek him." Hebrews 11:6.

The phrase, "the just shall live by faith," was the very phrase that lit up the reformation and brought to the world the light of the glory of the gospel more than five hundred years ago. The rituals of works to obtain salvation were exposed for what they were; useless rites. Thousands of people were released from papal superstitions that were only worthless inventions designed to turn men away from the simplicity of the gospel.

The reformation of the sixteenth century and onward sparked a blow to the reign of the papacy that she has yet to fully recover from. She will attempt to bring back the oppression and ignorance of the dark ages, but we are told in the Word of God that her power will come to a complete end. Anyone who aligns himself with the gospel is linked to the greatest power in the universe. He is linking himself with power that can storm the strongholds of evil and release the captives out of Satan's prison. The gospel has saving power and has time and time again proven that the grace of God is far more powerful than sin. It is one thing to read about the power of the gospel, but it is quite another thing to experience it in your own life. When the power of God is manifested in your life and salvation is a reality, it brings with it a force that the combined number of all wicked devils cannot stop. We have at our disposal, the power of God, and we would be foolish not to allow God to fight our battles in the conflict against evil.

There are many texts that could be mentioned to tell us about the way to receive justification and salvation, but there is one, that are the very words of our Lord and Saviour, Jesus Christ. This text is known the world over.

**"For God so loved the world, that he gave his only begotten Son, that whosoever believeth in him should not perish, but have everlasting life." John 3:16.**

It was God's love for every one of us in this world that moved Him to give us His only begotten Son Jesus. Nothing but the love of God should motivate us to seek for justification. Believing and trusting in Jesus brings us everlasting life. There is no other one that we can trust to save us from sin.

"And she shall bring forth a son, and thou shalt call his name JESUS: for he shall save his people from their sins." Matthew 1:21.

"Behold the Lamb of God, which taketh away the sin of the world." John 1:29.

It is Jesus only that saves us from the penalty and power of sin. It is Jesus that takes away the sin of the world.

The love, and mercy of the Father resulted in Him sending His most precious gift in the person of His only begotten Son Jesus to bear our sins in Himself. It was not an easy decision to make, but when God foresaw the fallen condition of man and his great need, He was moved with compassion. It was at a great risk that He sent the One that was always by His side, the One who was His equal, the One altogether lovely, the One who was His beloved Son. If only the heart of man would perceive and see the love of the Father and the Son for guilty man. Accepting and appreciating this would lead to a clearer understanding of the plan of salvation. If man so desired, his heart would be transformed and we would end misery and strife. Love would so permeate every vein and cause Satan to run for the exit. The armies of heaven would drive out the tyrant and no more prisons would exist. Man would become truly free and liberty would reach pinnacles that it has never reached before. Sin would end abruptly and we would forever be beyond its reach.

There is coming a day when this world will come to an end. When the followers of Christ reflect His loving and righteous character, He will recognize that fact by coming the second time to take them, His children home.

"And this gospel of the kingdom shall be preached in all the world for a witness unto all nations; and then shall the end come." Matthew 24:14.

We are promised that the gospel will go to the four corners of the earth and will be preached in all the world. The key part of the text says "for a witness." This witness is the character of Christ. When the world sees the loving and merciful character of Christ in His people, many will be convinced of the truth of the gospel and will receive it. They will then join the ranks of the people of God and will be saved and find entrance into the kingdom of God.

Let us let the reality of the gospel sink deep in our hearts. Let us see the love of God for a planet of rebels. Let us allow the gospel to do its work in us and we will be transformed from rebellion to obedience. We will love righteousness and hate iniquity. There will be such a revival of godliness in our lives that men will take knowledge that we have been with Jesus.

In receiving Jesus, we receive deliverance, salvation, eternal life, and freedom from the penalty and power of sin. Because of the peace and freedom that is promised to anyone that receives Jesus into his heart, there must not be any delay. How can we ignore so great a salvation? Receiving Jesus restores to us joy that the world cannot give and it certainly cannot take away.

The love that God has for us is stronger than anything else, and yet it does not force the conscience. We are given the freedom of choice. Our response to God's love is a choice. Satan is the one that uses force. So contrary is force to the government of God, that freedom of choice is the very nature of God. Do we choose the loving Jesus, or do we choose the tyrant Satan? Jesus brings true freedom from sin, peace, and eternal life. The tyrant brings only suffering, misery, pain, death, and destruction. The people of Christ's day chose Barabbas over Him. Do not make the same mistake. The Saviour is waiting to enter the throne room of your heart. Why don't you let Him in? If your life is one of misery, let Jesus in, and you will enjoy the peace that passes all understanding. You will enter upon an experience that is fulfilling and lasting. The blessings to be enjoyed are endless. You will have difficulties and trials, but these pale in comparison to the abundance of blessings that you will receive. The joy of the Lord will be your strength.

# Chapter Eight

# The Problem of Justification

A casual glimpse of the title of this chapter may lead some to believe that justification is a problem. It has this title because, if all that is done for the sinner is to declare him righteous, then it would be quite acceptable for him to go on sinning until Jesus comes. If all the sinner must do is to accept the justification and atonement that were accomplished through the life and death of Jesus, would there be a need for anything else? All the sinner would need to do was to have a mental assent to the atonement that was made. Everyone on the planet who mentally accepted the atonement would be forever beyond the possibility of being lost because the way would have been made so very easy because Christ suffered and we can rest assured that this was enough.

There are many who believe that because Christ suffered they are freed from obedience to the law of God, and they are free to go on sinning without end. There are many who would disagree with this and would deny such an accusation. But this is true because there are many who teach that all that needs to be done is to ask for forgiveness when they sin against God. Wait a minute. When has it become okay to keep sinning with impunity? When has it become quite the norm to just continue to hurt the heart of God by presumptuously assuming that Christ's sacrifice on the cross means license to live as one pleases?

Let us reason this out. We know that Christ came to do away with sin. The Bible's definition of sin is that it "is the transgression of the law." 1 John 3:4. For all of those who have been endowed with reasoning ability, wouldn't it be a logical thing for the ones who have accepted the sacrifice of Christ as the atonement for their sins to rid sin out of their lives? Wouldn't it be safe to conclude that if the guilt of sin wounded and pierced the heart of Christ to the point where it broke His heart so that He died, then the sensible and wise thing to do is to eradicate sin out of their lives? If sin is breaking the law of God, and Christ bore the guilt of all our sins, and suffered the strange but righteous wrath of God against sin, and voluntarily laid down His life for our sins, then it follows that sin cannot dwell in the presence of God. Moreover, there would be no purpose for the sufferings, and sacrifice of the Son of God for our sins if there is no future life in heaven? And if there is a future life in heaven where everyone and everything is perfectly holy, our lives are to conform to the atmosphere of heaven where there is no sin.

There is a sinister movement among many professedly Christian churches of today that teaches that God's law is no longer binding and necessary since it was nailed to the cross. Was the law of God really nailed to the cross? How could a person come up with such a conclusion? I dare say that this doctrine is from the monster of monsters. Satan is the one that leads men to think that the requirements of God's holy law are no longer a part of the government of God. The devil is the one that moves men to concoct such a blasphemous teaching. This error, or should I say sinful heresy, leads many to the conclusion that they can go on sinning without being accountable to neither God nor man.

If the law of God is really done away with, then sin is no more sin. This erroneous conclusion begs me to ask this question, "what was the purpose of Christ coming to die for our sins if the ten commandments are canceled?" Do you see the confusion that results from the teaching that the law is done away with?

Since we see that there is no evidence in the Bible to support this erroneous belief that God has no law to govern His subjects, we can now look at "the incompleteness of justification" more closely. Let us be fair. Perfection is a requirement in the Bible. Therefore, we are not to have any issues with it. In this context, perfection is justification or the process where God declares us righteous by crediting to us the perfectly righteous life of Christ. The reason why justification is incomplete, as much as we are completely freed from the record of our past life of sin, is that it only completes one phase of perfection which is initial perfection; where the justified sinner is declared righteous. The sinner who sees His own sinfulness, and by faith, accepts the sacrifice of Christ as the atonement for his sin, and then receives justification or forgiveness which declares him righteous in the eyes of God, has started out on the road that will end in him going home to live with Jesus when He comes the second time.

The journey to heaven has specific road laws that must be followed if there can be any hope of completing the journey. But if someone comes along and tells you at the beginning of your Christian journey that the road laws are really not necessary, then one has to conclude that it is insanity to come to such a conclusion.

When we drive along the busy streets, we see road signs or laws posted all over. They are designed to protect us and other drivers, passengers, and pedestrians against injury, loss, and death. Can you imagine the carnage that would occur if there were no speed limits or stop signs? I know you get the picture. There would be such disaster that there would be no guaranteed safety in venturing out on the roads. The probability of you dying on the roads would be raised to astronomical proportions. Insurance rates would skyrocket, and road injuries and death would multiply. If drivers are already breaking the road laws even though road signs are present all over, can you imagine what would result if the local and state governments declared that there are no more laws to govern motorists? There would be public outrage and the authorities would be made to answer for such an insane declaration.

So, it is with the law of God. His laws are no arbitrary declaration, but they were designed to protect us from totally unnecessary and unjustified suffering and eternal death. The ones who teach that there is no more law are being continually deceived by Satan. He was the first preacher who taught men that God did not mean what He said about man dying if he disobeyed His commandment. God commanded Adam and Eve, in the Garden of Eden, not to eat the fruit from the tree of the knowledge of good and evil. Satan came along and preached a short sermon to Eve telling her that God really did not mean what He said and there would be no harm in eating the innocent looking fruit. He twisted the truth that God had spoken by saying that Eve would not surely die if she ate it. Satan was really saying that this law against eating from this tree was not binding. Do you see the parallel?

**Preachers all over the world are repeating the deception that was in the first lie ever recorded in the Bible by saying that God's law is done away with.** This teaching is so illogical that I cannot wrap my mind around understanding how a person endowed with reason can utter such blasphemy. The ones who teach such a thing should spend some time to ponder such a thing. Have you ever done something really ridiculous and afterward realized how unwise you were for having done it? Well, I believe it would be a wise thing for preachers who teach such a doctrine to really ponder on their conclusions to see the utter foolishness of such a teaching which is deception. It is Satan who is behind it all because He utterly despises the law of God. He refused to acknowledge the laws of God in heaven and taught other angels to disregard them and rebelled against God to the point where he lost the peace and happiness that was once his delight. He and the other angels who joined him in his hellish enterprise were evicted and cast out of heaven. To cause men to be lost is his goal in influencing them to teach that the law is done away with.

Now that we have logically concluded that God's law is binding and necessary, let us look even deeper into why there is a problem with stopping at justification and not continuing on the road of perfection or sanctification. Justification is what puts us on the road of perfection, but many have been deceived into thinking that it is the whole journey and this is what is meant by "the incompleteness or problem of justification." There is no problem with justification or initial perfection as it is. It is flawless, and faultless. One of the man-made issues with justification is the faulty conclusion that many have made in thinking that it is the end of the journey and that the declaration of perfection is all that is necessary in obtaining entrance into heaven. Initial Perfection or justification is not enough to secure our assurance of going home with Jesus when He comes the second time. Justification is the first phase of the whole plan of salvation. We will deal with the second phase in chapters 14 and 15.

The justified sinner cannot grow in grace by just accepting the atonement and the justification that is credited to him by the perfect life of Christ. He must accept the other aspect of salvation which is sanctification. Continual obedience to the law of God is necessary for the candidate for heaven to be prepared to go there. He cannot go on sinning. He must not just be declared holy. He must be made holy. What proof do I have? It is this simple. Let us look at Revelation 22:14-15. It reads:

> "Blessed are they that do his commandments, that they may have right to the tree of life, and may enter in through the gates into the city. For without are dogs, and sorcerers, and whoremongers, and murderers, and idolaters, and whosoever loveth and maketh a lie."

Verse 14 says that a blessing is pronounced on those who keep the commandments of the Lord. The keeping the commandments of God is what gives one the right to enter into heaven when Jesus comes the second time. There can be no mistake about this. If a person wants to have the right to enter heaven, then he will obey God's law through the power of the Holy Spirit living in him. The next verse should dispel any doubt as to whether a person can go on willfully sinning until they die or until Jesus comes the second time. It says that those who will not obtain the right to be admitted into heaven when Jesus comes again are dogs, sorcerers, whoremongers, murderers, idolaters, and liars.

If accepting the atonement of Jesus was all that was necessary to make it into heaven then this verse would have never made it into the Scriptures. If a person is fair, unbiased, reasonable, and impartial, he will not hold on to the flawed idea that sin is ok in the sight of God. We have conclusive evidence from the above two verses and the rest of the Bible that sin is so offensive to God that it cannot be permitted to live in the souls of those who desire to go home with Jesus when He comes again.

We can therefore see the problem that would arise if all it took for a person to obtain the right to enter into heaven when Jesus comes was to only accept the justification that is freely offered and given to him. That person could go on with business as usual or sinning as usual. He could live as he pleases with no consequence.

The erroneous doctrine that tells us that God's law is done away with is one that has perverted the morals of society. The church is supposed to be the agency that God uses to save men from sin, but when this same church turns around and says that the standard or law that God uses to govern us is no longer in force or binding, can we expect anything short of the production of a society full of robbers, assassins, murderers, fornicators, adulterers, liars, disobedient children, sexual perversions, alcoholics, rapists, predators, monsters, drug dealers, drug addicts, "freedom fighters," segregation, racists, class warfare, oppressors, dictators, and a whole host of other evils and kinds of sinners too numerous to list. To say that God's law is done away with is to remove the only barrier that ensures the peace and safety of the citizens of any society. To declare that the law of God is done away with is to declare that you no longer have faith in the Bible.

Satan's objective in destroying faith in the Bible effectively makes void the law of God. This design of the devil is just as effective as destroying the Bible itself. And so, he has accomplished the same results that the world has seen from "the Dark Ages," when the Bible was suppressed. This period was one of lawlessness and prevailing spiritual darkness. It greatly impeded the progress and growth of whole nations and was responsible for the state of morals during that period.

However, the Reformation of the sixteenth century opened up the eyes of men to something more precious, lasting, and elevating. For the first time, many saw the light of the glory of the gospel and were transformed into beings that saw their real value in God's eyes. They became motivated to serve God, and in so doing their lives were transformed from sin to holiness. Their aimless lives now had new purpose. This is the power of the gospel. It turns a man into a gentleman and a woman into a lady. It transforms a sinner into a saint. It turns a robber into an honest man. It makes the drunkard sane. It elevates the mind to higher thoughts. The mind becomes more robust and stronger. Intellect grows to tremendous heights, and society benefits from men putting to use their God-given gifts and talents. The morals of society are greatly improved and crime and lawlessness retreat. The effects of receiving and practicing the law of God as outlined in the Bible produces a nation that causes the world to stand back and watch in awe as the hand of God blesses everything good that they undertake.

**In ministers preaching that the law of God is no longer necessary, they are essentially saying that they do not need to be made holy. They are quite satisfied in believing the lie that Satan tells them that because Christ died, His blood covers them, and it is enough, and therefore they are released from the bondage of the law. You read that right. These deceived preachers call God's law bondage. But isn't the law a protection against the bondage of sin?**

How is it that Satan has succeeded in deceiving and convincing men that keeping God's law is bondage? Do you see the senselessness of teaching such a thing? This is the height of ignorance. How did this come to be? It was through "the men of the cloth" and teachers of the Bible. It was through the very ones that claimed to be God's representatives and Bible instructors. They were the ones to sell such a lie to their unsuspecting congregations. It is amazing how men put their trust in finite man. The Bereans of Acts 17:11 knew better than the members of most churches in our modern world. Hear what this text says: **"These were more noble than those in Thessalonica, in that they received the word with all readiness of mind, and searched the scriptures daily, whether those things were so."** Yes, they received the Word with eagerness, but they did not stop at this. They verified if what Paul said was really what the Scriptures said. They also made sure about the interpretation. This is excellence and virtue.

Here we have a principle in dealing with doctrine. We are not just to be satisfied with the preaching of the Word and accept it and rest assured in it then and there and that is it. We are to move on to our own personal research of what the preachers and teachers teach so as to verify the truth. We are to follow on to know the Lord and the truth of the Scriptures for ourselves and not become a reflection of other men's thoughts. Have you ever been asked a religious question that you were not able to answer and told the person that you would ask your pastor and get back with that person to give them an answer? Have we as a society grown so dependent on ministers and Bible teachers as to trust our soul's salvation to them? They have no heaven to take us to nor any hell fire to cast us into, but we can allow them to influence us in deciding or choosing our destiny. Yes, it is true that we are to respect everyone, but that respect does not mean that we are to blindly follow these deceived ministers and teachers down the road to perdition and hell. Let us cast off this bondage of dependence on finite man and run to the Source of wisdom, knowledge and understanding who is Jesus. The Bible declares to us His character which is righteousness. Let us each choose wisely.

# Chapter Nine

# The Perfect Example of Perfection–Part I

In education there is theory and there is practice. The theory of education does not give us hands on training and is only partial education. The education that one receives is not complete if it stops at the theory. There must be some kind of practical training so that education is not lopsided. This balanced training comprising the theory as well as practical training result in a balanced education.

In the spiritual realm we have the theory of perfection also. We are told in Scripture to be perfect, but if all that we were taught was the command to be perfect, then we would be at a loss as to how it was done. To create balance, we are given the perfect example of how to be perfect in the person of Jesus, the righteous Son of the living God.

The doctrine that teaches that men can earn their way to salvation strikes at the very heart of the gospel. It does away with what God does for man and replaces it with man's works which, we know, are flawed and inadequate to meet the claims of the law of God.

If the works of man were enough to satisfy the holy wrath of God against sin, then he could atone for his sins, and there would have been no need for a Saviour. Man would have had the right to glory in his own works of righteousness, but justification casts down man's glory into the dust and it does for him that which he could not do for himself.

To save man from the penalty of sin Christ bore our sins and received the wrath of God against sin and his life was crushed out. To credit to man's account a record of perfect righteousness, Christ presents and gives us His perfect righteousness. His righteous life stands in place of the sinner's unrighteous life and he receives this imputed righteousness or justification and God looks upon him just as if he had never sinned once in his life.

The conflict of the ages between Christ and Satan has always been about the validity and fairness of the law of God. Satan had always cast contempt on the law of God. He claimed that God was arbitrary and He was just looking out for Himself and cared more about Himself than His subjects. This challenge to the law of God created such a division among the angels of heaven that God eventually rid heaven of Satan and the angels who joined with him in his rebellion.

Satan, who at first was named Lucifer before he abandoned his position of covering cherub, was the chief angel, next to Christ. God had created Lucifer with all the glory that He could, without him becoming God. He had all the power, glory, splendor, and might that a created being could possess without him having the immortality, omnipotence, omnipresence, and omniscience of God. He was created perfectly holy. Somehow, one day, he developed this strange feeling of pride in himself. This feeling of pride led him to become jealous of Christ, who was the only Being that could enter into close communion with the Father. Lucifer wanted the position of Christ so desperately that he allowed himself to be possessed by his own demons of envy, jealousy, malice, and pride. This strange feeling of pride, he did not dismiss, but he entertained, and it seemed to elevate him to new feelings of satisfaction in his own accomplishments, and his good looks. Next to the Father, Son, and Holy Spirit, he was the most exalted being in the universe, but this new feeling of pride caused him not to be satisfied with the position, natural beauty, and the gifts that God had endowed him with. He wanted more. Ever wondered why many rich men are always desiring more wealth when they have more than heart could wish?

Satan's challenge to the law of God led to open rebellion, and at least one third of the angels in heaven abandoned their own positions because they believed in the lie that Satan had told on God. He proclaimed that God's law was unjust. The seed of rebellion was sown and many were left in doubt as to whether Satan was telling the truth. His rebellion was a new thing and his accusations must be proved to be wrong or right. He must be allowed to demonstrate his claims. It must be proved that Satan's way of rebellion in casting away the divine laws of love and justice were not for the good of God's created beings and His government.

His claims must come to maturity so that his accusations could be tested as true or ungrounded.

Thus it was that Satan decided to commit himself completely to war against the government and rule of God. He trusted in his own way, and he, along with the angels that joined him in his rebellion, were expelled from heaven.

When God cast Satan and his evil angels to the earth, they found success among our first parents, Adam, and Eve. Every created being in the universe must be tested to prove whether they were loyal to God. The power of choice was given to our first parents, and we know the sad history; they both disobeyed God and lost their innocence. They were created perfect but fell into sin when they both ate the fruit from the tree of the knowledge of good and evil that they were expressly commanded not to eat from. Their nature went from perfectly holy to fallen and disobedient and they became subject to death. They naturally became rebellious against God and blamed God and the devil for their sins.

To save man from the pit of sin into which he had chosen to sink into when he disobeyed God, the promise of the seed was given in Genesis 3:15. "And I will put enmity between thee and the woman, and between thy seed and her seed; it shall bruise thy head, and thou shalt bruise his heel." This seed or offspring, was to save man from sin, but He was also to vindicate the character of God by demonstrating to the universe that the accusations of Satan were completely groundless and without reason. To accomplish this amazing and difficult task, the Son of God, who was equal with God, was to become a human. If he perfectly obeyed the law of God in His humanity, it would be demonstrated to the universe that it could be obeyed by man. In the Son of God taking on flesh, it would be shown that the Godhead was willing to subject themselves to their own law. Satan was not willing to subject himself to the holy and righteous law of God.

The whole universe watched in amazement and awe as the divine Son of God took on humanity and became a babe by the power of the Holy Spirit. Satan had succeeded in imbuing everyone that was ever born on the earth with fallen, and sinful human nature. When Jesus the Messiah came to this earth, Satan was thrown into confusion. Here was his former Commander, humbling Himself and taking on flesh or humanity. He had become like the beings He created. This mystery is too complicated for us to fully understand. How could the Creator of everything and everyone become like the beings He himself created? How could He, who was one with the Father, become like man in his fallen state. Christ took on sinful flesh with four thousand years of deterioration and decay. We are to have no misgivings as to the nature that Christ took on Himself. The sinful nature of man is not sin, because we have already established that **"sin is the transgression of the law." 1 John 3:4. A person sins by choice, not by nature.**

We could spend a great deal of time discussing the nature of Christ, but one thing is for sure; He became like us, and "was in all points tempted like as we are, yet without sin." Hebrews 4:15. This humiliation that Christ put on Himself was a most severe test. It was the ultimate humility. Christ covenanted with the Father to go and save man at whatever cost to Himself. This mission in coming to this earth was at a great cost and was a tremendous risk. If Christ should fail in perfectly obeying the divine law of God, Satan would be right in his claim that God was arbitrary, and his law was not designed for the good of His subjects.

The whole universe must witness the unmasking of the evil designs of Satan, and all doubts must be forever banished as to whether God loved His creation more than He loved himself. Every one of God's created beings comprising the angels, man, and the inhabitants of the other worlds that exist in the universe must see the demonstration of love that God has for them in the person of His Son living as a man on this earth. He was to subject Himself to suffering, ridicule, hunger, abandonment, betrayal, denial, and eventually death. All of this He saw before He became man. When Christ became man, He did not have any recollection or memory of who He was before He became a babe in Bethlehem. This knowledge of who He really was, and His mission, became known to Him while He was in His youth, because we read of His response to His earthly parents when they went looking for Him. "How is it that ye sought me? wist ye not that I must be about my Father's business?" Luke 2:49. He asked them if they did not realize that He must be occupied with carrying out His Father's business. He was busy doing the will of the Father who sent Him on the mission to save man from sin and the undertaking to vindicate the character of God that Satan had misrepresented.

In Christ taking on humanity, He was to show to man, that God's law can be perfectly obeyed. He was to show us how to obey God's law of love. The tempter must be met on His own ground. Satan claimed man as his because man disobeyed God when he sinned. Christ was to defeat him as a human being, and in doing this, rightful ownership and governing of man would be transferred back to God. If Christ lived a perfectly righteous life on this earth, He would show to us that we too, can be victorious over sin and live a righteous and holy life, free from willful sin.

When Christ came to this earth as a babe in Bethlehem, Satan knew who He was. His birth was different from every other human born on the earth. Christ's birth was by Mary, a young virgin, who was with child of the Holy Ghost. She did not get pregnant by any man, but the Holy Spirit placed Christ in her womb, and the Son of God was born a baby.

Satan's hatred for Christ was demonstrated to the world and the universe from the cradle to the grave. Lots of babies were murdered because He moved Herod the king to slay all the children in Bethlehem, and in all the coasts who were two years old and under. Christ's earthly parents, Joseph and Mary, were commanded to flee to Egypt to escape this death threat. Satan knew that Christ's mission was to defeat him and his unfounded claims against the government of God. He must defeat the mission that Christ came here to accomplish or he must pay for his rebellion and its baleful results.

The failure of Satan in trying to slay the young child, Jesus, did not deter him from trying in every way to either take His life or cause Him to sin at least one time. We are not given a lot of insight into the childhood of Christ, but we are told one thing that must be the goal of every youth in this age of rebellion against authority. "And Jesus increased in wisdom and stature, and in favour with God and man." Luke 2:52. This text has a lot that we can unpack and we could spend a great deal of time on just this one. He grew, not just physically, but his mind grew in wisdom. He was accepted both by God and man. His early life was looked upon with admiration, despite opposition, and no one could rightly accuse Him of doing or saying anything that was wrong. In fact, His thoughts were perfectly pure and elevated.

The sinless life of Christ's early life was a rebuke to His peers and this proves to us that even children, if taught and trained in the right way, can walk as Christ walked and live as He lived.

"Train up a child in the way he should go: and when he is old, he will not depart from it." Proverbs 22:6.

"I will instruct thee and teach thee in the way which thou shalt go: I will guide thee with mine eye." Psalm 32:8.

Luke 2:52 demonstrates to the world the benefits to be gained by parent's training children in the way of the Lord. In doing this, parents are giving their children the best education in this life in preparation for the life to come. If more parents would live out the principles of true education, society would not be in the state it is in. The claims that misguided preachers make that victory over sin is not possible would be quickly dispelled by the overwhelming demonstration of the character of Christ in the youth of today. But how different is the character of the majority of today's youth.

**The claim that no one can gain the victory over sin is a sure sign of defeat from the start. If a man decides that he cannot do something what more can be expected than that he will not do that thing? He has failed without even trying. And so it is with spiritual things. If man claims that it is impossible to obey the law of God perfectly, what more can be expected of him than failure? How can you expect to succeed without the mind to succeed? If no attempt is made to gain the victory over sin, then what more can be expected than utter defeat? It would by ridiculous to expect victory without effort. It is Satan that tricks men into believing that they cannot overcome sin. Victory over sin is possible through the mighty power of the Holy Ghost in us.** The next chapter will deal with the temptation of Christ in the wilderness and it will be shown just how He defeated Satan. We will see just how we are to meet temptations when Satan presents them to us.

Before Christ can set out on His mission to save man from sin and vindicate the character of God, He Himself must be tested to see whether He will stand true to God or be defeated by the temptations of Satan.

# Chapter Ten

# The Perfect Example of Perfection-Part II

The Commencement of Christ's earthly ministry or mission is recorded in the fourth chapter of the book of Matthew. We have recorded for us one of the most decisive events in all history. The destiny of man hung on the balances and the victory of Jesus would give us hope in the great conflict against evil.

"Then was Jesus led up of the Spirit into the wilderness to be tempted of the devil. And when he had fasted forty days and forty nights, he was afterward an hungered. And when the tempter came to him, he said, If thou be the Son of God, command that these stones be made bread. But he answered and said, It is written, Man shall not live by bread alone, but by every word that proceedeth out of the mouth of God.

Then the devil taketh him up into the holy city, and setteth him on a pinnacle of the temple, And saith unto him, If thou be the Son of God, cast thyself down: for it is written, He shall give his angels charge concerning thee: and in their hands they shall bear thee up, lest at any time thou dash thy foot against a stone. Jesus said unto him, It is written again, Thou shalt not tempt the Lord thy God. Again, the devil taketh him up into an exceeding high mountain, and sheweth him all the kingdoms of the world, and the glory of them; And saith unto him, All these things will I give thee, if thou wilt fall down and worship me. Then saith Jesus unto him, Get thee hence, Satan: for it is written, Thou shalt worship the Lord thy God, and him only shalt thou serve. Then the devil leaveth him, and, behold, angels came and ministered unto him." Matthew 4:1-11.

When Christ, the Messiah or the One Sent was about thirty years of age, He was baptized in the Jordan river. When this event happened, the Holy Spirit descended upon Jesus in a bodily shape like a dove. The Father's voice was heard from heaven saying, that Christ was His beloved Son in whom He was very pleased. Immediately after this, He was led up into the wilderness to be tempted of the devil.

When Christ was directed by the Holy Spirit to go into the wilderness, He spent forty days fasting and was in close communion with His Father. He must be endowed with power from on high to take on His adversary Satan. At every stage in His life, Satan was defeated and now Christ must face the same type of temptations that Adam and Eve had failed to overcome in the Garden of Eden. At this stage in the conflict between Christ and Satan, everything was at stake. Christ was to meet with the one who was once the most exalted being next to Himself in all the universe. If Christ was defeated in the wilderness of temptation, the whole plan of salvation and the vindication of the character of God would have failed, and Satan would have obtained full control of the mind of man. There would have been a reign of terror that would have engulfed the whole earth. The seeds of rebellion that Satan had sown would have grown to maturity. Anarchy and violence would have been the order of the day. Satan's claims against the law of God would have been right if Christ had failed in overcoming and defeating his temptations. He would have been correct in His accusation against God and Jesus saying that they created laws they were not willing to abide by.

Christ was led into the wilderness to contemplate the mission that He had undertaken. In fasting and praying, He was to obtain strength to meet the trials that He was to be subjected to. This would prepare Him for the way that He was to travel in saving man.

The forty-day fast of Christ in the wilderness is the example we need to strengthen us in this conflict that is being waged over who will reign on the throne of our hearts and who is it that will be master of our minds and whose bidding we will do.

There are several benefits that we receive from fasting. What are they?

1. It gives the digestive system a chance to rest

2. It clears the mind so that we can communicate better with God

3. It gives the body a chance to do needed repairs and maintenance

4. It gives one the opportunity to receive a clearer understanding of the Word of God

5. It causes one to have a greater appreciation of the Scriptures

6. It helps one to lose weight

7. Fasting helps to improve certain processes in the body

8. Fasting helps with prolonging life

9. It improves feelings of hunger

10. Fasting improves eating habits

11. Fasting causes us to feel better

12. It causes us to focus better on spiritual things

As Christ was locked in communion with God, Satan waited for His opportunity to tempt Christ. He must conquer Christ, but if He failed, Christ was to gain the mastery. Satan did not leave this warfare to be conducted by any of His imps. He himself was at the head of this conflict. When Christ was in the wilderness of temptation Satan saw this as a golden opportunity to tempt Christ to sin.

As we look into the temptation of Christ in the wilderness, let us look at a brief history from the book of Genesis to the time when Jesus was in the wilderness. Here it is:

1. God creates Adam and Eve perfectly

2. Adam and Eve indulge the appetite and eat intemperately

3. Man becomes alienated from God

4. God comes in search of man

5. Man hides himself from God

# THE PERFECT EXAMPLE OF PERFECTION-PART II

6. God cries out to man

7. God promises that man would defeat the serpent through His Son Jesus

8. Eve thinks that her firstborn son Cain was to be the Chosen One to defeat the serpent

9. Cain kills Abel

10. The human population multiplies on the face of the earth

11. Men become very violent and their thoughts become impure and wicked

12. Noah finds grace in the eyes of the Lord

13. God destroys the earth and only eight people are saved

14. Noah gets drunk

15. Esau sells his birthright for some food

16. Many of the Israelites perish in the wilderness because of the continual indulgence of their depraved appetites

17. Israel settles in Canaan but succumbs to self-inflicted wounds brought about by their rejection of God's laws

18. The book of Proverbs warns man of the dangers of gluttony, intemperance, the indulgence of appetite, and alcoholism

19. Daniel is a captive in Babylon but refuses to place in his system any food or drink that would defile him

20. King Nebuchadnezzar utters some of the most beautiful words in all the Bible after living on a diet of grass for seven years

21. The promised seed, Jesus, goes into the wilderness to be tempted of the Devil

So man fails to perfectly resist the onslaught of the serpent. Jesus, the only begotten Son of God, is sent to live out a perfect life of obedience to the commandments of God so that man might have the example of how to overcome in this warfare over the mind.

For God to vindicate His character, Jesus was to be tempted in the same way that Adam and Eve were tempted. If He failed this test, Satan would triumph.

After Jesus fasted for forty days, He became very hungry. To deny one's self of food by fasting for a reasonable period is essential in assisting him in gaining the victory over appetite. If Jesus who was sinless fasted, are not we supposed to follow in the footsteps of the Master in our quest to be victorious over appetite? The answer is yes. **(WE ARE NOT GENERALLY REQUIRED BY GOD TO FAST FOR FORTY DAYS AT A TIME.)** If this was so, then all the great men and women of the Bible would have fasted for at least forty days once in their lifetime. Sin has such a foothold on humanity that it is essential for us to fast for periods of time.

Did Eve fast from the fruit from the tree of the knowledge of good and evil? Sadly, she did not. Adam did not fast also. Jesus fasted from food for not just one or two days, but forty days. What an example for us! What self-denial, what sacrifice, what emptying of self! He did it, for not just the vindication of God's character, but for us also. The salvation and redemption of man could not be accomplished if Christ did not endure and pass the test of appetite.

When Christ was locked in communion with God, Satan was not permitted to interfere or disturb. This is a lesson for us. We are to be found in secret prayer and communion with God. "But thou, when thou prayest, enter into thy closet, and when thou hast shut thy door, pray to thy Father which is in secret...." Matthew 6:6. When we, in sincerity, truth, honesty, and purity, are in close communion and meditation with God, we are in the presence of God. "He that dwelleth in the secret place of the most High shall abide under the shadow of the Almighty." Psalm 91:1.

When Satan came to Jesus after forty days he was trying to obstruct the mission of Jesus to save man. As long as we are on this earth we will have to endure the onslaughts of the devil. If Jesus constantly faced the tricks and traps of the devil during His earthly life, we too, who are followers of Christ are to meet with obstacles, but we are to take courage in the fact that God has promised to be with us in the valley of trial and temptation.

"And when the tempter came to him, he said, If thou be the Son of God, command that these stones be made bread." Matthew 4:3.

After forty days the pangs of hunger were felt by Jesus. This was the opportunity that Satan was waiting for. Satan appeared to Jesus in disguise. He disguised himself in the Garden of Eden when he deceived Eve, and now He again disguises himself as an angel of light. **"And no marvel; for Satan himself is transformed into an angel of light." 2 Corinthians 11:14.** If Satan should appear as himself, many would recognize him and resist and flee away from him. But many are deceived by him because they do not see beyond the deception and disguise. How was Christ going to identify the wily foe? How was He going to come to the realization that it was Satan that was talking to Him? Was He going to give in to his suggestions or was He going to defeat him?

Satan's temptation that Jesus command the stones to be turned into bread, may have seemed, to some, like an innocent thing, but how often it is that the seemingly innocent and small things cause the greatest pain and suffering. Adam and Eve ate just "a nice looking fruit" and the world was plunged into woe that is too great to express.

> "Even so the tongue is a little member, and boasteth great things. Behold, how great a matter a little fire kindleth! And the tongue is a fire, a world of iniquity: so is the tongue among our members, that it defileth the whole body, and setteth on fire the course of nature; and it is set on fire of hell." James 3:5-6.

One of the reasons why Christ came to the earth was to take on humanity so that He could demonstrate to us how to overcome sin. Christ's response to this temptation is a lesson for us as to how we are to overcome temptation.

**"But he answered and said, It is written, Man shall not live by bread alone, but by every word that proceedeth out of the mouth of God." Matthew 4:4.**

**This is the answer. We are to resist Satan's temptations by the Scriptures. We must become familiar with and know key Bible texts so that when the temptation comes, we may be able to recall a specific text to deal with the temptation. But if we do not fortify our minds with the Word of God, we will not find help in time of need because we will not be able to call to mind a Scripture or Scriptures that will meet the temptation. Psalm 119:11 provides us with the antidote for temptation. "Thy word have I hid in mine heart, that I might not sin against thee."** We cannot store the Word of God in our minds if we do not study it. We study in school; we train our minds to grasp temporal things; many of us contemplate things that are of little value, and yet most of us fail to spend time in acquainting ourselves with the Scriptures that are able make us "wise unto salvation through faith which is in Christ Jesus." 2 Timothy. 3:15.

The Scripture Jesus repeated to the devil was found in Deuteronomy 8:3:

> "And he humbled thee, and suffered thee to hunger, and fed thee with manna, which thou knewest not, neither did thy fathers know; that he might make thee know that man doth not live by bread only, but by every word that proceedeth out of the mouth of the LORD doth man live."

The answer of Jesus was another signal blow to Satan; defeated again. God is never defeated in any instance. Good always triumphs over evil. "Be not overcome of evil, but overcome evil with good." Romans 12:21.

The example of how Jesus defeated Satan in this first temptation should inspire us with hope, faith, and courage. It should lead us to give thanks to God for giving us the solution in this great battle over who will be the master of our minds. When Satan disguises himself and so hides himself away from view when he tempts us, the Scripture is our safeguard. We can depend on it. The Word of God has never failed and will never fail. The Scripture gives us the assurance that we are not left to ourselves in this fight against sin, but we are more than conquerors. **"If God be for us, who can be against us?" Romans 8:31.**

The words of Satan to Christ gave him away. Satan's words, "if thou be the Son of God," were coined in such a way as to insinuate doubt in the mind of Christ. If Christ were to give in, He would have failed to demonstrate trust in God's testimony that He had just received about forty days before when the voice from heaven said, "This is my beloved Son, in whom I am well pleased." Matthew 3:17. Here Christ had the confirmation that He was indeed "the Sent of God." Our faith in God must rest on the Word of God, and it is in the Word of God that we are given a demonstration of the love of God for us. We are to rest in the Word, knowing that what God says He will do. We do not have to doubt the Word of God because it is the weapon of choice in defeating the devil.

Christ overcame Satan's first temptation in His humanity. He did not have the advantages that Adam and Eve had and enjoyed when they themselves were tempted by Satan. Their bodies were perfect and without any taint of the results of sin in the slightest degree. The disadvantages that Christ had to contend with are listed below:

1. Loss of access to the tree of life
2. Loss of access to the garden of Eden
3. Loss of the continual visible presence of holy angels
4. Loss of the ability of perpetual life
5. Loss of a sinless environment
6. Death of the vegetation
7. Death of the animals
8. Physical degeneration of the race
9. Man's lifespan significantly decreasing
10. The presence of crippling diseases
11. The constant temptation of Satan suggesting evil thoughts and actions

12. Man's evil attitude towards God

13. Man's view of the fairness, mercy, and love of God

The above list is by no means exhaustive but it gives us an idea of just how much more difficult it was to overcome sin when man's body was racked with the results of sin for over four thousand years. This should give us assurance that we too, can overcome sin, although the body of man has been plagued with the results of sin for thousands of years. We are to overcome sin by being connected with the Father, Son, and Holy Spirit.

When Satan came to Christ after the forty day fast, he did not know what was in the mind of Christ but he took notice of how weak Christ was after forty days. Satan is not allowed to read minds, but he notes our actions. He does not have the power of omniscience. If he did, he could go out and prepare his temptations to flaunt in our faces. However, he has studied the human mind for thousands of years. He takes note of behaviors, and habit patterns. He knows the weaknesses that we have and skillfully adapts his temptations to meet each individual case. If we were perseveringly determined to repress the sinful thoughts that Satan suggests, not giving them any heed in word or action, the enemy would, without a doubt be defeated. But how often it is, that we do not resist the suggestions and evil thoughts that come to our minds. We dwell on them and then we express them in words and actions. The result of this is that repeated words and actions turn into habits. This is how we ourselves determine where we will end up when Jesus comes the second time:

 -Thoughts lead to actions
 -Actions lead to habits
 -Habits lead to character

-Character determines destiny

Whatever we love to dwell upon in our minds is what is demonstrated by our words and actions. There must be constant meditation on holy themes. The mind must not be allowed to wander. Be determined to bring it back to the place where it loves to contemplate scenes of purity instead of scenes of impurity in all its forms. If you have a difficult time and find yourself dwelling on impure and perverted things, do not give up. Ask the Lord for a double portion of His Holy Spirit to overcome your evil thoughts. Choose to serve God. You will find that repeatedly resisting the suggestions and evil thoughts supplied by Satan will cause him to be overcome and defeated. You will love to dwell on holy things. As you do this, your life will be brought into harmony with God. People will notice the transformation of character because your actions will show the inworking and outworking of the character of Christ in you. The habitual actions repeated shape the character.

We are not to believe that one wrong act determines our destiny, generally speaking. This is not saying that it is alright to choose to sin even once. Sin is never an option. One wrong turn or sin could cost us our eternal life. We must avoid sin as one avoids AIDS or the big C. God does not wish for us to sin, but if we do sin, we must run to the Rock and be broken and contrite. Do not delay this. **(WARNING: WILLFUL SIN IS DANGEROUS AND COSTLY. BEWARE.)** God will forgive us our sin and cleanse us from all unrighteousness. We must forsake the sin that overcomes us or it will get the better of us. We are not to give up in dismay and tell ourselves that we cannot gain the victory, because we can overcome all known sin through the power of God in us. Even the good deeds we do are not to be occasional. They are to become an integral part of us and something that has become a pattern and habit. The habitual deeds or misdeeds determine character. As we form characters like Christ or Satan, we demonstrate to God, the world, and the inhabitants of heaven and the other unfallen worlds who our real master is. We will then be rewarded with a place in heaven or we will die an eternal death.

**Adam and Eve were overcome by Satan's temptation to indulge the appetite. Christ's first temptation in the wilderness was the temptation to indulge the appetite. The severity of this temptation is demonstrated by the long fast that He endured. Praises ought to go up to God for the victory over appetite that Jesus obtained in the wilderness of temptation. Jesus overcame because He surrendered His whole life to the control of the Holy Spirit. We too can defeat temptation by allowing the Holy Spirit to be on the throne of our hearts. With God all things are possible.**

## Chapter Eleven

# The Perfect Example of Perfection-Part III

The devil did not just give up because he failed to entice Jesus into sinning against God by listening to his subtle suggestions. Too much was at stake to just give up this struggle so Satan resorted to other temptations in his quest to get Jesus to break the law that He Himself gave to man.

Verse 5 of Matthew 4 says that the devil took Jesus to Jerusalem and placed Him on a pinnacle of the temple. For the Creator to allow His greatest enemy to transport Him to the temple in Jerusalem was a sight to behold. This was humility to the fullest. Christ was not to demonstrate His divine power on behalf of himself although He knew that it was Satan that transported Him to the temple. Let us picture this scene. Imagine how the holy angels must have been at every step in this journey to make sure that their Master was safe. However, Satan could not do anything to their Master without God's permission. Jesus rested in peaceful repose, trusting His very life to God. We are to do the same. We are to rest in the sweet assurance that God is our Protector regardless of the situations and circumstances we may find ourselves in.

Again Satan tried to get Jesus to doubt His true relation to God. He tried to get Jesus to prove that He was the Son of God. He suggested that Jesus throw himself off the pinnacle of the temple. Satan is a bold and an in-your-face foe. He will suggest things for us to do that are clearly stupid. My question is this: why would Jesus have wanted to throw Himself off the pinnacle of the temple? Sometimes you hear about or see things people do and wonder at the utter ridiculousness of their decisions. You ponder people's decisions and conclude that they have lost their minds to have done such things. I tell you, when a person is without Jesus reigning supreme in his heart, he is liable to do things which are clearly insane.

**Christ was not to place Himself needlessly in the way of temptation. He was not to be presumptuous and behave as if He could do anything that was not based on truth, and still have the abiding presence and protection of God and His holy angels. Christ did not of Himself go into the wilderness of temptation. He was led into the desert by the Holy Spirit. So it is with us: we are not to place ourselves in situations where it is clear that God did not put us there. Many a man has had confidence in himself and tried to parley with the enemy, thinking that he was strong enough to resist temptation, only to find himself succumbing to Satan's invitations and deceptions.**

Joseph, the son of Jacob, did not trust in his own strength to resist the temptation to have a moment of sensual pleasure.

> "And it came to pass after these things, that his master's wife cast her eyes upon Joseph; and she said, Lie with me. But he refused, and said unto his master's wife, Behold, my master wotteth not what is with me in the house, and he hath committed all that he hath to my hand; There is none greater in this house than I; neither hath he kept back any thing from me but thee, because thou art his wife: how then can I do this great wickedness, and sin against God? And it came to pass, as she spake to Joseph day by day, that he hearkened not unto her, to lie by her, or to be with her. And it came to pass about this time, that Joseph went into the house to do his business; and there was none of the men of the house there within. And she caught him by his garment, saying, Lie with me: and he left his garment in her hand, and fled, and got him out." Genesis. 39:7-12.

He used the hands, and legs that he was endowed with from His Creator to get him out of the presence of the seduction of Mrs. Potiphar. He did not say that he would stay in her devilish presence and that God was able to shield him from lusting, but decided that the only safety for him was to flee from her. How is it with this generation? Are the youth of today so connected with God in such a way that they will resist the temptation to lust after the opposite sex, or are they presumptuously playing with the fire of temptation thinking that they will be shielded from committing fornication? It is a fact that if we give the enemy any advantage, he will exploit it and before we know it, we are entangled in his web.

Today, we have available the internet. It is a way of conducting business, and a way of obtaining information quickly. It has revolutionized life in such a way that many of the methods we use to use in doing everyday things have become obsolete. It is a great tool to make life easier. But I wonder why they call it the internet and the worldwide web. Look at the name, the internet. We ought to be so very careful of the things we hear and the things we see. We are not to decide that we are strong enough to resist the sights and sounds of evil in all its forms that are found on the internet but we must say like David, "I will set no wicked thing before mine eyes." Psalm 101:3. Let us be very careful what we hear and what we see. We must not allow our ears to presumptuously hear sinful sounds and we must not allow our eyes to look on, contemplate, and ponder sinful things. Our minds are to dwell on things that are pure and holy.

What about alcohol? Many are lured into its net thinking that they will just drink a little at a time and that they are strong enough to resist the urge to get drunk. But this kind of moderation leads to a desire for more alcohol and before you know it you become addicted to this poison. You then fool yourself that nothing is wrong with drinking because of the addictiveness and deceptiveness of alcohol. This poison is such a deceiver that those who drink it will think that it is ok while they are ruining themselves.

When Jesus was tempted by the devil in the wilderness, he suggested that He cast Himself down from the pinnacle of the temple because God would have immediately intervened to prevent Him from injury or death by dispatching His angels. Again, Jesus responded to this temptation of Satan by saying that, "It is written again, Thou shalt not tempt the Lord thy God." Matthew 4:7. Scripture is the solution to every temptation, no matter how alluring it may seem. The text that Jesus here quoted is found in Deuteronomy 6:16. "Ye shall not tempt the LORD your God." Reference is here made to what the Israelites did in Massah and Meribah because of their chiding and because "they tempted the Lord, saying, Is the Lord among us, or not?" Ex. 17:7. The Lord had delivered them with a strong arm out of slavery and worked miracles of salvation in their midst and now, with ingratitude, they were tempting Him. They doubted God and put Him to the test. The Israelites were in a harsh desert and were being tested, but many of them failed to trust God.

How is it when we are in trouble? Do we rest in sweet repose and reflect upon God's mercies towards us in the past, knowing that He will take care of us in our present situations and circumstances, or do we needlessly whine and complain to God and man about our ordeal? Trust in the power of God means everything to us if we are to form righteous characters fit to appear in the presence of the King of kings. The unbelieving and doubting that many exhibit and entertain will not find entrance into heaven when Jesus comes.

When Satan quoted, or rather, partially quoted from Psalm 91:11-12, he omitted the words "to keep thee in all thy ways." This artful deceiver made sure that he did not suggest anything that would cause him to be at a disadvantage in his temptation. He maximized the deception and used his mastermind to construct the wording in such a way to produce deception. This phrase means to protect and preserve us in all the ways that God has chosen. "And lead us not into temptation, but deliver us from evil." Matt. 6:13. We are to go wherever He leads, and stay away from the ways of the wicked. We are stay on the path of loyalty and obedience to God instead of demonstrating a lack of trust in God by going in the way of the unrighteous.

There are many preachers who will quote only Scriptures that will sustain their erroneous beliefs, and will omit the ones that clearly oppose and defeat their false theories. They have presumptuously ventured upon the same ground that Satan used in this second temptation to compel our Lord to sin against God. We do not want lies or half-truths to defend any Bible doctrine. We are to judge things by the weight of evidence we find on any given subject. Because a text may seem to contradict other texts on the same subject is no reason to hold on to the one seemingly contradictory text. We are to trust God that it is no contradiction and study deeply and intently until the truth of the text is found out. God's Holy Spirit will guide us and lead us into all truth. "But the Comforter, which is the Holy Ghost, whom the Father will send in my name, he shall teach you all things, and bring all things to your remembrance, whatsoever I have said unto you." John 14:26.

When we hold on to a text to support a false doctrine or teaching that seems contradictory, the real problem is with ourselves. It is possible that this could be a result of a person's ulterior motive. It may also be the result of not fully trusting in God's Holy Spirit. It may be we do not trust in God's Word fully, we lack wisdom, knowledge, and understanding, we are ignorant, stubborn, rebellious, or deceived. We dwell upon the supposed contradiction instead of asking God to show us the real truth. We do not realize that when we do this, we are giving in to the same kind of temptation that Satan brought to Jesus and we deceive ourselves and others.

The issue of false doctrines is plaguing the Christian world. One of the main false doctrine that has caused a great deal of confusion and misdirection is the issue concerning the validity of the law of God. There are many who state that the law of God was abolished at the cross of Christ. The proponents of this erroneous view try to use Scriptures to back up their arguments for this false view and only use those texts that appear to support their views. They will misinterpret and misconstrue Bible texts, and in the process, lie on the Word of God. They deceive themselves that they are right and reject the testimonies of other Scriptures. They do not see that it is Satan who is inspiring them to believe his deceptions and sell lies to others, and are unsuspectingly drawn into his net. Our only safety is in trusting fully and completely in God and His Word.

Thus it was that Satan failed in his attempt to deceive Jesus into falling into the sin of presumption by casting Himself down from off the pinnacle of the temple. Satan now resorted to desperation to compel Jesus to sin. In his anger and frustration, the wily foe now attempts to get Jesus to worship him.

Let us not forget that Satan did not appear as the devil to Jesus but disguised himself as an angel of light. Satan again took Jesus up into an extremely high mountain and showed Him all the glory and splendor of the world's magnificent kingdoms. The dazzle, splendor, and glory of the kingdoms of this world were displayed to Him and Satan thought to use this to allure Jesus to sin.

This last temptation was the boldest yet that Satan approached Jesus with. The first two Satan challenged Him to prove His divinity and put God to the test. But this one went beyond and offered

Him a promise of the kingdoms of this world and the glory of them. The condition of receiving these kingdoms was to do "one simple act" of worshipping Satan. This was very bold, and daring. Who was he that he should offer the kingdoms of this world to Jesus on condition of worshipping him? Can you see the object, aim, and aspiration of Satan in rebelling against the authority of God in heaven? It was the worship and adoration that was given to God that He lusted and thirsted after. He was not interested in doing the will of God although he was the brightest, the most decorated, and the top brass among all of God's creation. He was not satisfied with this position. He understood that it was only Divinity that was to be worshipped. He was so against this that nothing was allowed to deter him from his desire for the worship and adoration of the angels in heaven.

Satan wanted the One who created him to worship him. How could this be? That is the boldness and shamelessness of the devil.

> "For by him were all things created, that are in heaven, and that are in earth, visible and invisible, whether they be thrones, or dominions, or principalities, or powers: all things were created by him, and for him: And he is before all things, and by him all things consist." Colossians. 1:16-17.

Could Christ, who carried out the will of the Father in creating everything and everyone in the universe stoop to do such a thing? How could the Creator worship the created? Friends, this is the boldness and blindness of sin when it is allowed to take up residence in one's heart. It blinds one to the things that are contrary to the will of God, and it leads one to do things that are clearly senseless, foolish, and worthless. Sin does not bring lasting happiness, peace, and joy, and it leaves one unsatisfied and disappointed. Sin may excite the passions, emotions, and feelings, but it also, in the process, weakens the mental, physical, and spiritual faculties. Its nature is to degrade and destroy. A person may feel temporarily and momentarily excited and "satisfied" when they commit sin, but sin acts like a drug. The more you do it, is the more you desire more of it. Sin can elevate you to an emotional high, and excite the passions, but then it also leaves you disappointed and unsatisfied.

**Satan himself is not satisfied with the worship of his victims. There is no trace of lasting peace, joy, and happiness in him. He has "no rest day nor night." Revelation 14:11. He can do no better because he has been utterly forsaken of God, and his evil traits have been developed to the maximum. There is nothing in him that can respond to the love of God, and his empty soul is void of anything that is noble and elevating. It is impossible for him to ever be at peace with himself or anyone else. He is the most wretched and miserable person in the whole wide world. He is jealous of anyone that he sees who possesses the loving character of God and he bends his effort to cause misery, pain, and death. He is the destroyer, and he works to bring ruin upon man. We cannot fully understand how much hatred Satan has for God and us. We cannot risk venturing upon his enchanted ground and expect to be safe. He has a death squad and he has ordered a hit on you.** Hear what Job says about how close he came to being consumed by Satan as much as he did not venture into his forbidden territory. **"I am escaped with the skin of my teeth." Job 19:20.** If Job, who was a righteous man, said this, there is no safety in going into enemy territory. Listening to forbidden music, beholding forbidden scenes, feasting on unhealthy foods, going to questionable places, keeping company with the licentious, all tend to work our ruin. We do not want to become a victim of the devil by choosing to be in his company, but we want to run to Christ the Rock of Ages. There is safety with Him. **"The name of the LORD is a strong tower: the righteous runneth into it, and is safe." Proverbs 18:10.**

Satan is constantly seeking fresh victims to be initiated into his hellish and sinister designs. He hates Christ with perfect hatred. If he could, he would drag our God off His throne. If allowed to have his way among men he would immediately commence his work of evil to pit man against man in worse ways than we have seen or heard about. He would bring upon the earth worse disasters, suffering, ruin, and death which would be seen everywhere and in a thousand forms.

The book of Job conveys to us just how angry Satan is against the child of God. As soon as God removed his hand of protection from Job's family and possessions, how quickly houses, livestock, children, and servants, were destroyed. Satan maximized the shock and awe that he received. In each instance where Satan wiped out Job's possessions and his children, he spared only one who witnessed it to go and tell him. The first one came and told him, and while he was telling him, another one came with more devastating news. While the second messenger was giving Job the bad news, another came and gave him more dreadful news. The devil reserved the worst disaster for last. All his children were killed by a very ferocious wind, and a fourth messenger delivered the news to Job while the third messenger was giving him bad news. Satan is the most extreme opportunist, and if allowed he will intensify the pain, misery, and suffering he brings upon us to the highest. I thank God that we have a Father who shields us from the maliciousness and hatred of Satan. We owe everything to God for the love and protection He gives us. We have the protection of holy angels sent from heaven to those of us who shall be heirs in God's eternal kingdom.

In Satan suggesting that Jesus worship him so that he would be given the kingdoms of this world and the glory, he was not telling the truth? Did he have the legitimate power to give Jesus the kingdoms of this world? Was he the one that was in charge of this world? Did he create this earth? Who is the real owner? The Bible states that "the earth is the LORD'S, and the fulness thereof; the world, and they that dwell therein." Psalm 24:1. How could he give what was not his? This was barefacedness and brazenness. It is like someone entering into a business enterprise or partnership with another. They both agree that the profits would be equally split between them. Somehow, one decides to cook the numbers in such a way that he gets the majority of the profits through deception. One day, the one who cooks the books decides that the time has come to buy out the other unsuspecting business partner with the money he stole from him. The unsuspecting one agrees to sell him his portion of the business. The business is now fully owned by the one who stole his money. The crooked business partner used the other's own money to buy him out. How cruel and devious is that man! To use another's money, and use it to do this cruel act, is the height of wickedness. The unsuspecting business partner gave his unscrupulous business partner a part of his fifty percent share of the business enterprise for free. Ever heard the saying that goes something like this, "you used my own fat to fry me?"

Yet, this is exactly what Satan did when he made the offer to Jesus. The earth was not his to offer because he did not create it. God is the rightful owner. But such is the nature of sin. Sin is a deceiver, and whoever meddles with and dabbles in it is opposed to Christ and uses God's resources, time, energy, gifts, and talents to perpetuate the aims of the enemy of God and man. All our natural endowments are given to us by God, and to use our God-given gifts to support the devil's kingdom is ingratitude in the highest sense. To willfully sin against God is to worship at the devil's feet. We are paying homage to the prince of devils. When there is a citizen of a nation who conspires with another nation, we call it treason. Satan wanted Christ to commit treason against His own government. Our only safety is in abandoning sin. Treason is an act that is punishable by death or imprisonment in the countries of the world.

**Have you committed treason against God by willfully sinning against Him? Have you given your best and youthful years to Satan? If you have, know that the time has come for you to cast off the works of darkness and throw your whole weight on the side of God. There is mercy with Him, and He will by no means cast you out if you sincerely repent of and forsake your sins. You will immediately pass from death to life, and from the kingdom of Satan to Christ's eternal kingdom.**

Satan's offer to Christ was one that involved eternal consequences. If Christ caved in, the whole plan of saving man and vindicating the character of God would have been unraveled and destroyed. This was the real object of Satan's temptations that he brought to Christ in the wilderness. His aim was to thwart the plan that was laid out before the foundation of the earth. If Christ worshipped Satan, he would have immediately become the ruler of this earth, and man would have been plunged into a reign of terror that would have intensified and there would be scenes of oppression, pain, and anguish than no pen could describe nor any mind fathom or understand.

I thank God that Christ did not give in. Satan was exposed for who he really is. He is the usurper and the deceiver. He hates God and man. He is the originator of sin. He has been deceiving men into sin for thousands of years. The results of sin has plagued this earth from Adam until now. I thank God that we have the assurance that the devil's reign of terror will come to an abrupt end and the time will come when "the saints of the most High shall take the kingdom, and possess the kingdom for ever, even for ever and ever." Dan. 7:18.

Worship is the privilege of the created directed to the Creator. Jesus, who is our perfect example of perfection directs us to "worship him that made heaven, and earth, and the sea, and the fountains of waters." Revelation 14:6. Christ responded to the devil's temptation by saying "Get thee hence, Satan: for it is written, Thou shalt worship the Lord thy God, and him only shalt thou serve." One of the Old Testament equivalent to this is found in Deut. 6:13 which says "Thou shalt fear the LORD thy God, and serve him......." The context of this text tells us that we ought to worship God only and no one or anything else. To worship anyone or anything else is to turn aside from the Lord.

Satan tried three times to lure Jesus into sinning against God and three times he failed. Thus it was that he failed to cause Jesus to sin and ruin the plan of salvation. At the answer of Christ in this third temptation, he was forced to flee because divinity flashed through humanity because the power of the Holy Ghost came upon Jesus. At the words of Jesus, "get thee hence Satan," he was compelled to flee. Sin cannot stand in the presence of divinity and it was for us that Jesus spoke these words. When Satan approaches us with his temptations, we are to use the Scriptures to combat his onslaughts. We are not to cower in fear of him who was cast out of heaven, but we are to boldly display the triumphs of the cross of Christ. Jesus is our defense and the Scripture is our safeguard.

Satan fled from the command of Christ and immediately angels came to minister to Him. He was thus strengthened to meet the task of saving man. This test in the wilderness was a signal defeat of the enemy. Let us live with the assurance that just as how Christ overcame every temptation, we too can resist temptation and obey God's law by the power of the Holy Ghost in us. Let us thank the Lord that we are not left up to ourselves to fight in this warfare of good versus evil, but "we are more than conquerors through him that loved us." Romans 8:37.

# Chapter Twelve

# The Perfect Example of Perfection–Part IV

Christ came to this earth to bear the sins of the whole world and to clear the path that had been obscured by sin. He came to also correct the wrong view of men toward their heavenly Father. Satan had painted God as being a tyrant and an exacting taskmaster. To sweep away these wrong views was the object of Christ in living among us.

Now that Christ had passed the test in the wilderness, He set His face towards the mission that He was to carry out. The Bible states that Christ went about doing good because God was with Him. He fully yielded His will to His Father and was endowed with the full measure of the Spirit of God. Nothing that Christ did was for his own benefit, but everything He did was in some way connected to the plan of salvation and the vindication of the character of God.

The nation to which Christ came was at that time, mostly ignorant of the fact that the time had come when the Messiah was in their very presence. The people were so blind that they could not see that the prophecies of Daniel 9, among others, concerning the Messiah, were being unfolded before their very eyes. They were so focused on earthly and material things that they were not prepared to welcome the King of kings to their nation. Christ came to His own and His own received Him not.

Christ worked miracle after miracle to prove to them His true identity, and His love for them, but they did not understand His mission to save them. He manifested Himself in a humble and unassuming way. There were few who had welcomed Him at His birth, and it was strangers in Jerusalem who brought gifts to Him when He was born. Mary and Joseph had to flee with the young child Jesus to a foreign country to escape the quest for His death. Christ's early life was one of toil, hardship, trial, and discipline and yet "learned he obedience by the things which he suffered." Hebrews 5:8.

When Christ began His earthly ministry at the age of about thirty, He gathered about Him twelve men who were to be His chosen disciples to assist Him in His mission to save man. He revealed to them the fact that He would go to the cross and die and rise again three days later. They did not understand this, and Peter, the most outspoken of the twelve, grabbed a hold of Jesus on one occasion and protested Christ's prophecy of His own death.

The cross, to the Jews meant something totally different from how modern man views it. The cross in the time of Christ meant one thing and one thing only. It meant death. When they saw anyone bearing the cross, they knew without a shadow of a doubt that

that person was being led to his place of death and nothing could stop that fact. The disciples of Christ were devoted to crowning Jesus King of the Jews. They believed that He would free them from Roman rule, but when He told them the reality of Him dying on a cruel cross, they did not pay attention to Him. The devil is a skillful general who creates distractions so that men will focus on one thing when the very thing that is needful to strengthen and protect them from his snares are ignored and even treated with disdain. If they only understood Christ's mission of redeeming man from sin, they would have grasped more of what He was trying to teach them. They loved Jesus vehemently but they did not understand His mission.

Christ spent three years dispelling the darkness of sin that had blighted His creation and brought pain, woe, and death to the inhabitants of the earth. As the time approached that He should go to the cross and suffer a cruel crucifixion, He set His face steadfastly to go to Jerusalem and word got around that He was coming to the city. As much as He was to suffer as a criminal although He had done nothing wrong, He was to be also honored as a King. He accepted the worship and adoration of the Jews when He made His triumphal entry into Jerusalem. The Jews were filled with hope, delight, and expectation as He made His way into their city. Along the way they waved palm branches and spread their outer garment on the path that He rode. Their joy knew no bounds as they saw Him whom they thought was to deliver them from the bondage and captivity of the Romans.

But Jesus's mind was focused on His mission. As He approached Jerusalem, He wept over it. He saw with the eyes of prophecy what would happen to the city because they would reject and crucify

Him who was their only hope. He did not linger around them for long because they would try to crown Him king by force. Opportunity came and He quietly got away from the presence of the lately elated and ecstatic throng.

As the night approached when Jesus was to be arrested and tried, He and his disciples made their way to the place where He had often retired to so that He could engage in prayer with God His Father. A sudden burden came upon him and every step he took was with labored effort. His soul began to be troubled as He slowly made His way to the garden of Gethsemane.

As Christ was in the garden He chose three of His disciples and took them with Him.

> "Then saith he unto them, My soul is exceeding sorrowful, even unto death: tarry ye here, and watch with me. And he went a little further, and fell on his face, and prayed, saying, O my Father, if it be possible, let this cup pass from me: nevertheless not as I will, but as thou wilt. And he cometh unto the disciples, and findeth them asleep, and saith unto Peter, What, could ye not watch with me one hour? Watch and pray, that ye enter not into temptation: the spirit indeed is willing, but the flesh is weak. He went away again the second time, and prayed, saying, O my Father, if this cup may not pass away from me, except I drink it, thy will be done. And he came and found them asleep again: for their eyes were heavy. And he

left them, and went away again, and prayed the third time, saying the same words." Matthew 26:38-44.

The sorrow that Christ felt was no ordinary one. He who voluntarily took upon Himself the task of bearing the sin of the whole world, was now being crushed out by it. Satan was suggesting doubts to Him. The guilt of man's sin caused such mental anguish to Him that was beyond human comprehension. It appeared as if the task of saving man was going to end in defeat.

As Christ knelt in prayer in the garden, His sweat was not normal during that night of agony. "And being in an agony he prayed more earnestly: and his sweat was as it were great drops of blood falling down to the ground." Luke 22:44. The Son of God was so filled with the burden and guilt of man's sin that He had volunteered to bear, that it forced blood through His skin. Three times Jesus begged the Father to remove the cup of woe from Him and three times Jesus submitted to the will of the Father. The victory had been gained. Jesus fully submitted to the will of the Father and decided that He would do whatever it took to save man from the penalty of sin.

We too must go with Jesus to the Gethsemane. **"Then said Jesus unto his disciples, If any man will come after me, let him deny himself, and take up his cross, and follow me." Matthew 16:24.** If we are to gain the victory over sin and perfect Christian character, we must take up our own cross of surrender and follow Jesus. Christ, our perfect example of perfection, did not have to surrender any sin because He did no sin, but He demonstrated to us what victory over our selfish nature looks like.

He showed us what it takes to overcome sin in all its forms. We are never called to bear the sins of the whole world, but we are called to have fellowship with Christ in His sufferings. **"We must through much tribulation enter into the kingdom of God." Acts 14:22.** The path to heaven is not for the faint of heart, the fearful and the unbelieving. Every man must count the cost of salvation and decide whether this is the path that he desires and is willing to travel. If he decides that he does not want to go that route then he has chosen to be destroyed by hell fire.

The perfectly righteous life that Christ lived out while He was here on earth has been demonstrated to us to inspire us with hope in following the path of the denial of self and fellowship in His sufferings. Submission and the total surrender of the will to God is the path to heaven. Christ lived a perfect life, so we too can refrain from willfully sinning against God. We are to trust God to do His perfect will in us. We are to allow Christ to perfect His perfect character of righteousness in us.

# Chapter Thirteen

# Fabricated News

"Fabricated news" is an expression that refers to news that is made up or false. It may be concocted for deception. It may be found in the long-established sources of news like the newspaper, magazines, television, radio, media outlets, the internet, etc. Fabricated news has no foundation in the truth. It is offered to the public as facts and accurate. It may be used to destroy someone's reputation.

The origin of fabricated news goes way beyond a few thousand years and takes us out of this world and transports us to the home of the God of the universe. The originator of fabricated news, Lucifer, who became Satan or the adversary, did not have any foundation for his propaganda. He himself, deceived himself, and believed that he had entered upon a higher, better, and more satisfactory sphere of living. He insinuated his doubts and stealthily passed it on to other angels. He accused the government of God of manipulation for selfish ends. His smear campaign involved painting God as being overbearing, and arbitrary. His accusations were baseless, and were borne out of jealousy of Christ. He also came to believe that the homage given to God was to be given to him and he went forth to spread fabricated news in the heavenly courts.

Great was Satan's power to deceive. He took the simple facts and twisted them with artful perversion. This he then presented to the angels of heaven in such a way as to assassinate the character of God. He gained a large following among the angels of heaven by spreading fabricated news about God. He was the first character assassin. He was the first murderer. He is the father of fabricated news.

This adversary has not changed his cunning ways and it is a fact that he was the one who introduced fabricated news to Adam and Eve in the Garden of Eden. All he did was to simply twist what God had told Adam with a promise of a better sphere of living and a wiser way of life. God had said that in the day that they ate from the tree of the knowledge of good and evil they would surely die. Satan came along and entered the serpent. He spoke with a charming voice and used fabricated news to deceive an unsuspecting Eve. Satan inserted one word into the exact words that God had spoken, and claimed that God was trying to prevent them from being as gods, knowing good and evil. He promised that they would become wiser by just eating the forbidden fruit. This one word changed the meaning entirely. God had said, **"Thou shalt surely die."** Gen. 2:17. Satan cunningly said' **"Ye shall <u>NOT</u> surely die."** Gen. 3:4. And so fabricate news and outright lies were believed to be truth and this plunged the whole world into woe too much to describe. The results of believing fabricated news continue in our day.

Listed below are just some of its results:

   1. Satan, who rebelled against the authority of God, con-

vinced at least one third of the angels in heaven to believe his deceptions, and in so doing they lost their positions in heaven and are held in chains of darkness, reserved for hell fire that will burn them up. Satan himself will be destroyed because he deceived himself by believing himself, and in doing this deceived untold millions and billions of angels and men.

2. Eve believed the disinformation that the devil spoke and convinced her husband Adam to join her in disobeying God. This is the origin of sin on the earth.

3. Cain believed that He could bring another kind of offering to God and still be accepted by Him. When his offering was not accepted, he took it out on his brother whose offering was accepted by God. He ended up killing his brother. It was Satan who tricked him into believing that he could offer whatever he wanted by suggesting that he do so.

4. Satan again tricked the people in Noah's day into believing that God would not destroy them. Fabricated news, again insinuated itself, and most men fell for this lie.

5. Satan deceived men into thinking that they could not trust the promise of God that He would not again destroy the world by a flood and so they attempted to build the first skyscraper but abandoned the evil enterprise when a strange phenomenon took place at this tower.

6. The devil moved God's chosen nation to reject Jesus the Messiah, and they ended up crucifying the world's Redeemer.

In what major ways does the devil use fabricated news in our day? In keeping with the subject of the perfection of Christian character, it is necessary to look at the counterfeit ways of salvation that are being preached by the popular churches of today. Many there are, who teach that God's law is not binding. They have no biblical basis for such a lie, but misinterpret and misconstrue certain texts to support their favorite theories. These ministers and teachers, pass their theories on to their congregations and they accept their lies or fabricated news as being true.

One of the most daring lies that Satan has convinced men to believe is the one that states that a person cannot get victory over sin. Ministers and teachers use Bible texts that are misinterpreted and misconstrued to convince themselves and others that perfection of Christian character is not possible. Satan has great success in this area and fools many into thinking that when Jesus comes, He will simply change them from sinners to saints. There is, however, no such teaching in Scripture. We are to gain the victory over sin in this life if we are to go to heaven with Jesus when He comes again.

Many are convinced that the blood of Jesus covers them in such a way that they can go on breaking God's commandments without any consequences for their heaven daring belief.

Multitudes deceive themselves into thinking that the seventh day Sabbath is Sunday instead of Saturday. This is one of the greatest fabricated news stories that Satan has deceived man with. The Sabbath celebrates God's creative and redemptive power, but in observing Sunday as the so-called Lord's Day, many are convinced that it is the true Sabbath, not realizing that it was Satan who moved the Romans to establish Sunday as a day of rest contrary to Scripture. The Sabbath is a sign of sanctification.

> 'Moreover also I gave them my sabbaths, to be a sign between me and them, that they might know that I am the LORD that sanctify them. And hallow my sabbaths; and they shall be a sign between me and you, that ye might know that I am the LORD your God." Ezekiel 20:12, 20.

Sanctification is the part of the Christian's journey to heaven that the popular churches have a problem with. Satan has extreme hatred for the Sabbath and so convinces men to trample upon it and make it void.

The deceiver has yet another doctrine that is diametrically opposed to the doctrine of perfection or holiness. It is the "once saved, always saved" doctrine. It teaches that once a person accepts the salvation of Christ it is impossible for him to lose it. There is no possibility of that person being lost and going to hell because he is immune against eternal death. They are safely in the arms of Jesus. The deceiver well knows that accepting this fabricated news story will ultimately lead men to sin against God or they will not strive to fight the good fight of faith and surrender their wills to God so they can gain the victory over sin.

Another doctrine that is opposed to the Bible doctrine of perfection is the one that teaches that when a person dies, they immediately go to heaven. The Bible says that "the living know that they shall die: but the dead know not any thing, neither have they any more a reward; for the memory of them is forgotten." Ecclesiastes 9:5. If when a person dies, he goes to heaven; it does not matter whether he lived a godly life; he will inherit eternal life anyway. This doctrine of the immortality of the soul at death contradicts one of the plainest statements in all the Bible. It reads:

> "For this we say unto you by the word of the Lord, that we which are alive and remain unto the coming of the Lord shall not prevent them which are asleep. For the Lord himself shall descend from heaven with a shout, with the voice of the archangel, and with the trump of God: and the dead in Christ shall rise first: Then we which are alive and remain shall be caught up together with them in the clouds, to meet the Lord in the air: and so shall we ever be with the Lord." 1 Thessalonians 4:15-17.

The above text states that when Jesus comes, He will resurrect the righteous dead. The saints who are alive when Jesus comes, will, together with them, be caught up to meet Jesus in the air, and so shall they all be with the Lord forever.

Satan has convinced man that they can trust in their preachers and teachers to interpret the Bible for them and so they set themselves up to be manipulated by fabricated news that is an instrument of Satan to carry out his plan to cause their eternal doom and death. Multitudes are lost who could have been saved if they did not commit their eternal life to a minister or Bible teacher. They were deceived into thinking that they did not have to study the Bible for themselves. This is what the Bible commands all of us to do. "Study to shew thyself approved unto God, a workman that needeth not to be ashamed, rightly dividing the word of truth." 2 Timothy 2:15.

It was Our Lord and Saviour who commanded us to "search the scriptures; for in them ye think ye have eternal life: and they are they which testify of me." John 5:39. Is it any wonder why many people in this world who claim to be Christians, are for the most part, ignorant of the important truths and teachings that are essential to their salvation and feel quite at home in this world! They are busy with trivial and worthless matters, and are caught up in the hustle and bustle of modern living. The cares of this life absorb their time and many would rather watch a movie than study their Bibles. If this kind of careless, and reckless attitude of indifference continues, it will eventually lead them to the point of no return where it becomes impossible for them to be saved when Jesus comes. May the light of the glorious Gospel of Jesus Christ lead us to see the need of vigilance, watchfulness, and complete soul surrender so that Christ can live out His perfect life of righteousness in us. We will be led into a life of holiness and righteous living.

# Chapter Fourteen

# Perfection-Part I

This chapter takes us into the second realm of perfection called sanctification. **In this realm of perfection, the sanctified saint moves from an era where he is declared righteous through the process of justification to an era where he is righteous through the process of sanctification or holiness.** This sanctification or perfection is where the repentant sinner or the justified saint lives the victorious life and where he is allowing Christ to live out His perfect life of holiness in him. Staying in the realm of sanctification requires care and caution. The sanctified Christian will not boast of perfection but will walk in humility before God and man. He will not boast that he is saved but will, in meekness and lowliness, ascribe all the power and glory to God for giving him the power to live a righteous life. He will not reach a point where he will say that he is beyond the power of sin and it is impossible for him to fall, because his dependence is not on himself but it is on the Lord who sanctifies him. As much as perfection is required, the child of God will remain dependent on Him. He realizes that it is God that gives the desire to be righteous, and he is empowered, strengthened, and preserved by the power of the Holy

Spirit dwelling in him. He does not do good deeds to be seen, but he quietly and unassumingly does works of righteousness.

Christ worked miracle after miracle while He was here on earth. His life was one of continual service to man. Everywhere He went He spread the sweet fragrance of heaven and men were the recipients of His rich, heaven-sent blessings. Christ did not toot His own horn like the self-righteous religionists of His day who would often be heard making their loud prayers in the streets. As much as Christ's life was one of perfect righteousness, He did not seek to bring attention to Himself or brag about His accomplishments and natural endowments. The godly character that was the very core of His life was seen by men and they could not help but notice. Christ did not make His light shine but He let it shine. His life was not one of forced obedience to God and a painful struggle to keep from sinning, but it was one that was the perfect outworking of the power of the Holy Spirit in Him.

When a person is in the realm of sanctification, he is considered perfect in God's eyes. He is not perfect in the sense that he has no sin whatsoever, but perfect in the sense that he is not willfully sinning. He may slip and fall rarely, but this is the exception, not the rule of his life. You see, character is not decided by the occasional good deed or bad deed but it is determined by the general direction in which the person goes in; whether he is reflecting the character of Christ which is demonstrated in his righteous life or whether he is reflecting the character of Satan by living an unrighteous life of sin. If the sanctified saint sins, he is sorry for hurting the heart of God, confesses his sin and repents of it. It grieves him that he has sinned against his Maker and craves restoration into the divine image of holiness. It is the Holy Spirit's work to convict us of sin and in so doing we are given the power to turn from our sins if this is our earnest and true desire and will. We can choose to serve God and in so doing we are empowered to repent and do righteous works.

Many there are, who look on the subject of perfection as one that involves perfect sinlessness. Let us clear up the confusion that has resulted from a wrong understanding of what perfection is. When some people hear the word perfection, they immediately think that the individual who is perfect has no sin whatsoever in his life. However, a better way to look at perfection, is to view it as a condition of refraining from willful sinning. The individual is experiencing Christian growth and His character displays the fruit of the Spirit. He does not seek to disobey God, and he hates sin. God lovingly and patiently reveals to the sanctified one the sins that he commits that are in opposition to His law. God does not overwhelm him with a revelation of all his sins that he is ignorant of all at once, but he shows them to Him and in a way that he will not be driven to despair. If God should reveal all our sins at once that we commit that are against Him, many of us would give up in dismay and decide that it is impossible to live a righteous life; but He knows us better than we know ourselves. He tenderly and mercifully unfolds to us our sins, faults, and defects in the most tactful and timely ways. This does not in any way excuse a person being willingly ignorant and trying to avoid knowing what the sins are in His life. The Bible is within the reach of everyone. We are to search it for ourselves to know what truth and

**light is. The Bible reveals to us our sins and shows us the way how to overcome them.**

The person who obeys God willingly is perfect in His eyes. The individual who willfully sins against God is imperfect in His eyes. So, anyone who accepts the atonement that the plan of salvation offers has passed from death to life and is admitted into this process of sanctification if he chooses to live a life that is Christlike and different from the world. The person who is sanctified is perfect at every stage in sanctification. Today God may reveal to him some sin that he is unknowingly doing. He repents of and forsake this sin, gains the victory over it, and then, at another time, God reveals another sin that he is committing. If that person continues to humble himself and allow Christ to do of His good pleasure, He will find that His life is one of continual victories over the sins that God reveals to him. If he slips and falls, he quickly gets up, brushes off, and continues in this journey of the perfection of Christian character or sanctification.

Just what is sanctification? It is the process of being made holy or righteous. It is the process of perfecting Christian character. It is Christ who pronounces the child of God as being perfect and not the child of God himself. "If I justify myself, mine own mouth shall condemn me: if I say, I am perfect, it shall also prove me perverse." Job 9:20. "And the LORD said unto Satan, Hast thou considered my servant Job, that there is none like him in the earth, a perfect and an upright man, one that feareth God, and escheweth evil?" Job 1:8. God declared that Job was perfect. There is nowhere in the book of Job that Job declared himself perfect. Trusting in one's perfection invokes feelings of pride and arrogance and disqualifies one from being pronounced perfect by God. The perfection that is demonstrated in the life of the true Christian is the result of Christ dwelling in him and he cannot claim any righteousness or perfect living that is inherent in him. The good deeds that he does and the righteous life that he lives are the results of Christ living out His holy life in him.

We have already established the fact that if all Christ did for us was to justify us or forgive us of our sins, then we could go on sinning continually until we die or until Jesus comes and there would be no need of being made righteous. It is so essential that we understand the process of sanctification so that we can make an intelligent decision as to whether we are willing to make the sacrifice that is necessary in order for it to become a reality in our lives. If all that happens in a person's Christian life is justification or initial perfection then these sad words will be heard, "depart from me, ye that work iniquity." Matthew 7:23. Just so that it is clear as to how a person gets to sanctification we will here go through the process. This is it:

1. The law of God is the great standard that shows us our true condition. We have broken the commandments of God. We have sinned.

2. We recognize our need of a Saviour, and we cannot save ourselves by our own works.

3. Christ bore our sins in His body on the cross and delivers us from the penalty of sin which is eternal death.

4. We become convicted of our sins when we "Behold the Lamb of God, which taketh away the sin of the world." John 1:29.

5. Jesus bearing our sins in Himself gives Him the right to be our advocate and intercessor before God on our behalf.

6. Through Christ we now have access to God's throne of grace and mercy.

7. We repent of our sins through the saving power of the Holy Spirit and are sorry for bringing such pain, guilt and anguish to the innocent Son of God and we are sorry for sinning against God and the Holy Spirit.

8. We confess our sins to God and trust in the grace of God believing that we are forgiven.

9. We are immediately justified and God looks on us just as if we have never sinned once in our life because the perfectly righteous and sinless life of Christ is credited to us and our sinful record is erased. This process is justification or initial perfection.

10. As much as we are justified and initially made perfect through the process of justification, the problem of the old man of sin in our lives must be dealt with. As soon as we are justified, we immediately move into the process of sanctification or continual growth in holiness. (Sanctification keeps justification current.)

Just how is a person sanctified? Just exactly how are we made perfect in God's eyes? How do we experience Christian growth? How do we gain the victory over sin?

## PERFECTION-PART I

<u>The Bible is clear on the need for the children of God to be sanctified or made holy. Sanctification is what prepares us to go to heaven to appear in the presence of the King when He comes the second time. Sanctified reasoning tells us that Christ paid the penalty for sin so sin must be a very heinous and abominable thing in God's eyes. And if sin is a heinous thing, then it cannot dwell in His presence. So, before we can enter into the Holy City, sin must be eradicated and uprooted from our lives. To teach that we cannot gain the victory over known sins in our lives is to teach that God cannot supply us with the power we need to overcome sin. And if God cannot supply us with the power that we need to overcome sin, then there is no point in even receiving justification because we are justified first in order to be sanctified. And if we are not justified, then the life of Christ is of no benefit. And if the life of Christ is of no benefit, then His death for our sins was in vain. Without sanctification and the perfection of Christian character, the whole plan of salvation to save us is unnecessary, and a failure. To oppose victory over known and willful sin and and to oppose perfection is to choose the second death. Victory over known and willful sin is the perfection of Christian character.</u>

The false doctrine that teaches that it is impossible to gain the victory over sin is one that deceives men into thinking that they will be given a free pass into heaven in spite of, and despite their sinful lives. They claim that the blood of Jesus covers them and so there is no need to have victory over sin and it is impossible to gain victory over it. What can you expect from someone who claims that victory over sin and perfection of Christian character is impossible but only failure to gain victory over sin and the perfection of Christian character? This is failure from the beginning because that person has decided to fail. Because they have decided to fail, they try to enter into heaven another way. This will never work. "Verily, verily, I say unto you, He that entereth not by the door into the sheepfold, but climbeth up some other way, the same is a thief and a robber." John 10:1.

A person cannot be justified without being sanctified, and he cannot be sanctified without being justified. Justification is our title to the celestial city called heaven, and sanctification is our fitness for heaven. Justification is given to us on condition of our future obedience or compliance to the law of God at conversion and sanctification is the process of being made holy by obedience to the law of God after the conversion experience. A righteous character is developed through sanctification. Justification does not develop in us a righteous character but it prepares us to develop a righteous character.

Let us pretend for a moment that you are trying to get to a certain destination. You must travel on two specific roads to get there. There is no other way to get to your destination. The name of the first road is Justification Avenue. The name of the second road is Sanctification Highway. You cannot get to the second road without first traveling the first road. If you end your journey on the first road you cannot get to the second road and if you do not complete the second road you cannot get to your destination. This destination is called heaven. If you try to get to heaven another way you will find that it only ends at the precipice called Disaster Cliff. The only way to obtain eternal life is through Jesus because

He says, "I am the way, the truth, and the life: no man cometh unto the Father, but by me." John 14:6. The only way to get to our Father who is in heaven is through Christ and Christ brings us justification and sanctification.

Stopping at justification keeps us here on earth and does not perfect our character. Justification is one part of the whole picture. Moving on from justification to sanctification put us on the road that ultimately leads us in through the gates into the celestial paradise called heaven.

There are many ways in which we can liken sanctification and justification. One very good example of these two processes is this. They are the wings of a bird. If a bird has only one wing it is impossible for that bird to fly because it is just not balanced enough to become airborne. So it is with us. We cannot have proper Christian growth if either one is absent.

Most Christians, if not all, have no problem with justification because it is forgiveness of sins, and the perfectly righteous life of Christ is substituted for our sinful lives. However, sanctification is quite a different story. It requires a sacrifice which most people are not willing to make. Many prefer to hold on to tradition, culture, religion, family, personal preference, instinct, and impressions, instead of submitting to God so that He may do His perfect will in him. Sanctification requires the giving up of the self life and receiving the life of Christ. It requires a man to give up the sinful attractions, distractions, and diversions of this world.

It is truly shocking that sanctification which is the means of obtaining heaven when Jesus comes the second time receives such universal pushback and opposition. Sanctification fits and prepares us to be qualified to enter into heaven. If only the mind of man would reason that God's way is the best way. The temporal things that this world has to offer pale in comparison to the incentives and rewards that God presents and offers to us. We are not to be paupers. We are not to be wasting away in hunger, but we are to become children of the King. Heaven is worth it. Choose it today.

# Chapter Fifteen

# Perfection-Part II

How is a person made perfectly righteous or sanctified? The process of sanctification is of the utmost importance and demands our study. We know that destruction awaits those who continually reject knowledge, so it is imperative that we familiarize ourselves with such a process. The Bible provides the answer as to how a person is sanctified, victorious over sin, and how to keep justification current.

**Justification is kept current or up to date by sanctification. If we desire for God the Father to continually justify us or to ever look at us just as if we have never sinned, we must participate in the process of sanctification. When a person first receives justification, it is given on condition of his future obedience to God's law. This obedience is in the realm of sanctification. This future obedience is the obedience of the saint after he accepts the justification of Christ. It happens in the realm of sanctification. It is the sanctified life that the converted sinner lives after he comes to Jesus in repentance, confession, and justification. This future obedience is not**

in the distant future but begins in the immediate future following these three processes.

There is to be no delay in living the sanctified life because tomorrow is not promised to anyone. We are not to delay and put off obedience because it can be fatal. Additionally, why would you want to delay something that brings you an abundance of immediate and future blessings that are priceless. The Bible does not say "tomorrow;" it says "today" and it also says "now." "For he is our God; and we are the people of his pasture, and the sheep of his hand. To day if ye will hear his voice, Harden not your heart......." Psalm 95:7-8. "For he saith, I have heard thee in a time accepted, and in the day of salvation have I succoured thee: behold, now is the accepted time; behold, now is the day of salvation." 2 Corinthians 6:2.

The Lord in His great mercy has provided for us a means by which we can be fitted for heaven. This means involves denying self and following Jesus to the experience of death to self, akin to the one that He experienced in Gethsemane. For a person to come after Jesus or become His disciple, Christ Himself stated that He must "deny himself, and take up his cross, and follow me." Matthew 16:24. For the character of Jesus to become ours, we must be partakers in the life He lived, involving the continual denial of self, and the taking up of the cross or yoke of total surrender.

The text above tells us emphatically and unequivocally, that if we want to be like Jesus in character, we must participate in a life of the denial of self that Jesus lived. There can be no crown without a cross.

Just exactly what does the cross represent? Jesus also talked about the yoke. The cross and the yoke are symbols which both represent the same thing. The cross or yoke is the giving up of the will. The will is the power of choice or the power of decision. There must be total and complete submission or surrender of the life and whole being to God. The cross or yoke is not to be confused with the trials that we go through. Many have mistaken the meaning of the cross mentioned in Matthew 16:24. How do we know this? In the days of Christ, when He was here with us, when a criminal was seen carrying his cross, it meant only one thing, and that is, he was about to be crucified. We are not required to carry a physical cross to physical death, but we are required to surrender our self-life and give our wills to God so He can sanctify and make us righteous. The old man of sin must be killed or crucified. Self must die. There can be no Christian growth in sanctification or perfection if self is alive. Christ's example of total surrender in the Garden of Gethsemane is what everyone who is being sanctified must experience for himself in order to have growth in sanctification.

We all must die the death that Jesus died in Gethsemane which involved total and complete surrender to the will of God. Jesus said, "O my Father, if it be possible, let this cup pass from me: nevertheless not as I will, but as thou wilt." Matthew 26:39. This death principle is what many professed Christians have a problem with. They want to live His life without dying His death. This poses a great problem. No one should seek to evade his personal cross. This is not talking about a physical cross, but it is the one that results in burden bearing and a life of service. We are to be ever willing to carry out the will and wishes of Christ. Evading the cross is denying Jesus. He sacrificed all for us. We are to be willing to sacrifice all for Him. We are surrendered to Christ when we give Him complete control of ourselves. We are to be completely dead to our sinful nature, and the pangs and urgings of temptation will not overcome us. It is as if they do not exist. This principle of death to sin is the truth that has been hidden from many by Satan, as he would have it.

As much as the physical cross that Christ died on is a symbol, the reality of the cross of submission is even more important. We are continually sanctified when we are daily surrendered to Jesus. No one can be fitted for heaven without dying to self. "Verily, verily, I say unto you, Except a corn of wheat fall into the ground and die, it abideth alone: but if it die, it bringeth forth much fruit." John 12:24. Jesus is here telling us of the absolute necessity of the experience of death to self, which is the death of the old man of sin. The repentant sinner must fall on the Rock, Christ Jesus and be broken. The self-life must be crucified.

The process of the death of man's sinful nature is compared to a grain of wheat falling to the ground and dying. In the natural world this process is indeed a miracle, because, before the grain of wheat is planted or sowed, it lies dormant in storage. There is no growth or life when it is stored away, but when the farmer plants or sows it in the field or farm, it dies and a new life springs up in the form of a plant. This is a mystery that can only be accepted because we do not know exactly how the grain of wheat dies in the soil and results in a new plant. One thing we must accept, and that is the fact that it is the power of God that produces the growth of a new plant from that grain of wheat that was in storage.

This new plant that is produced by the grain of wheat that was planted or sown, fittingly represents the process of sanctification or the Christian growth process because the plant grows in stages.

> "And he said, So is the kingdom of God, as if a man should cast seed into the ground; And should sleep, and rise night and day, and the seed should spring and grow up, he knoweth not how. For the earth bringeth forth fruit of herself; first the blade, then the ear, after that the full corn in the ear." Mark 4:26-28.

We can see, that for eternal life to be given to the justified sinner, he must enter into the process of sanctification. The old self-life or the old sinful nature must be buried and stay buried. It is a fact that the dead know not anything, so, as long as the old man of sin stays buried, there is continual victory over sin in the new life that is produced as a result of the process of the continual death of the old man of sin. Death produces life. It is only the power of God in the justified saint or the repentant sinner that produces the new life that is sanctified by Christ through surrender.

There can be no evading of the crucifixion of the old man of sin. Self-centeredness which lies at the root of man's rebellion against God must be sacrificed on the altar and the will must be surrendered to Christ.

The reason why there are so many false doctrines that pervert the doctrine of sanctification is man's stubborn determination to bypass the sacrifices it involves. The denial of the self-life is required, bearing one's cross is a must, and the surrender of the will is indispensable.

What is the will? It is the power of decision or the deciding power in the mind of man. The will is the power of choice. It is not the taste, nor is it the inclination. It is not man's instincts. The will is not the feelings, passions, or emotions. It is given to us by God. It is ours to use or exercise. The power of choice is a powerhouse that can be either used for good or evil, or for blessings or curses. The choice is ours. Have you ever done anything in your life that you regret and wish that you could undo? The things we do, whether good or bad, are done as a result of the will or the power of choice. We choose to do what we do. **Note: We are not to mistake will power with the power of the will. Will power is determination and exertion. The power of the will is the power of decision or the power of choice.**

It is this will that God wants. **"My son, give me thine heart, and let thine eyes observe my ways." Proverbs 23:26.** This is the work of God in us. God so desires for you to surrender the power of decision or the will to Him so that He can be in control and Christ can be the only King on the throne of your heart. When Christ is in control He can then live out His perfect life in you which brings all kinds of spiritual blessings.

The surrender of the will is the great problem of man. He naturally hates the things of God. "Because the carnal mind is enmity against God: for it is not subject to the law of God, neither indeed can be." Romans 8:7. The carnal mind or the old man of sin cannot be reformed, adjusted, improved, renovated, or cleaned up. There is only one thing that can be done with it. This carnal mind is the unregenerate mind or the mind that refuses to change or reform. It is opposed to God. It is in opposition to the things of God and it can never be subject to the law of God. The only solution to this carnal nature or this stubborn old man of sin is that it must die. Without the death of this miserable old man,

Christian growth and victory over sin are impossible. When the old man of sin is buried, and stays buried, eternal life springs up in the born-again believer.

The reason why there is so much woe, pain, suffering, and sin in the world is the result of this stubborn old man. This old man can be referred to as man's selfish nature of sin. The natural motive of sin is selfishness. All selfishness is sin and all sin is selfishness. The reason why men willfully break God's commandments is due to the presence of selfishness in him. The old man of selfishness cannot be forgiven. God is willing and ready to forgive sins, but this old man of sin or the carnal nature must be crucified or put to death. This is the solution to the problem of sin. If the old man is crucified and stays crucified, then there is victory over willful sinning.

A person who has the experience of victory over sin may slip and fall into sin, but this is the exception, not the rule of his life. We are fallen and weak as mortals, and it is only when we keep the old sin nature dead and buried that we have continual victory. However, if we resurrect the old man we slip and sin. The sanctified saint who makes a mistake and sins against God, recognizes his sin and quickly repents and forsakes it. He does not willfully practice sin because he is born of God.

There is a lot of confusion in the Christian world as to how God looks on sin or treats it. Some teach that all that is necessary for us is to ask God for forgiveness when we sin and we are thereby safe and saved. As long as we continually confess our wrongs to God, He will forgive us. This kind of teaching and practice lead men to continually sin against God, and think that God will tolerate and even look kindly upon their continual transgression of His law.

The Bible is in direct opposition to this kind of mindset. There can be no victory over sin as long as men allow themselves to be tricked by deceived preachers who teach this kind of doctrine to their congregation. It only confirms them in their wrong doing and wicked acts, and perpetuates the pain and woe in the world. If the men who teach others this false and blasphemous doctrine do not repent, they will receive the wrath of God. They will be punished more severely than the ones they caused to sin because they claimed to be God's mouthpieces or spokesmen. Standing between God and man is a great and solemn responsibility and many do not understand how much of a duty is placed upon them.

Another way in which man is confused as to how God looks at sin or treats sin is with the doctrine of "once saved, always saved" as previously mentioned. It teaches that once a person receives the gift of salvation he cannot lose it. It teaches that he cannot fall from grace and if he does experience a fall, it is because he never did receive the gift of salvation by faith in Jesus in the first place. Can you see the natural result of such a daring blasphemy? It leads men to live as they please without being accountable to God. It puts man in a false sense of security, and leads men to think that everything is ok because they have mentally accepted the death of Jesus as the atonement for their sins. This teaching has millions in its grip and millions have been deceived into thinking that they can go on sinning without any consequences.

These two false doctrines are opposed to the true doctrine that teaches that the perfection of Christian character is required, possible, and necessary.

In looking at victory over sin, I have come to the conclusion that some of the confusion that results from the subject of perfection is that many look at Christian perfection as being a condition in which the perfect saint's record after he becomes a Christian is absolutely free of any sin whatsoever. The Bible does not teach this at all because it records the sins that even righteous men of old have committed. What made the difference was that they did not remain in their sins but they repented and abandoned them. They shook off their sins and again were restored to the connection they had with God and gained victory over sin. The perfect Christian does not claim perfection, but God sees his perfection. God sees that he is practicing righteousness and God recognizes that fact by giving him a fresh endowment of His Holy Spirit every day. The perfect Christian's life is one of continual victory rather than one of continual defeat.

Here what the Bible says in 1 John 2:1. "My little children, these things write I unto you, that ye sin not. And if any man sin, we have an advocate with the Father, Jesus Christ the righteous." It is the will of God that we do not sin and that we have victory over sin. To not sin is to live a life of victory over sin. However, if we make a misstep and sin, we are not to wallow in our sin and bemoan it to the point where we are in despair, but we are to be confident in the fact that we have someone who stands between us and God so that He will forgive our sin against Him. The text says "if we sin." It did not say "when we sin." If it said "when we sin," it would imply that it is ok to go on sinning because we have an advocate with the Father. The Bible does not condone sin, but recognizes the frailty of man. It does not excuse sin but it gives man the opportunity to make a clean cut away from it.

The goal is to gain the victory over every known sin that so easily beset us. We are not to keep on failing to gain the victory over the same sin repeatedly. However, failure is not a reason to give up. We are to run to Jesus for the power we need to overcome sin. Satan knows our weaknesses and he exploits them. When he sees that we fall into the same sin over and over again, he brings the same temptation over and over again. If we resist him, he will flee from us. The thing is, tomorrow is not promised, so I want to take advantage of the opportunity today.

If a person continually falls into sin over and over again, he has not the joy of victory over sin. The reason why he is an addict to sin is that he is not surrendered to God. Surrender does not mean defeat. In fact, surrender is the opposite of defeat. Surrender is victory over sin, because, when a person is surrendered to Christ, it is He that now lives out His perfect life of righteousness in him. As long as Christ is living out His perfect life of righteousness in him, he will not fall. The fall occurs when he willfully and deliberately takes himself out of this life of surrender. The soul must consent to dethrone Christ from the throne of his heart and then he commits willful sin. It is, however, not a safe thing to willfully sin because one cherished sin can and will cause eternal death if not repented of and forsaken. The Bible records men who dabbled and played with sin and how they paid for it with their lives. Sin is not something that is our friend. The consequences of sin are real and not something to be desired. If the disease of sin is not gotten rid of, it will wreak havoc in the soul. Not only will it wreak havoc in the soul, but it will lead to eternal death.

The perfection of Christian character is a teaching that must be understood and accepted as a possibility in this life, and not some distant thing that the saved will experience when Jesus comes the second time. Perfection is our privilege to enjoy here and now.

We must believe in such a possibility. We must wear the robe of Christ's perfect righteousness here on earth.

# Chapter Sixteen

# The Possibilities of Perfection-Part I

Wonderful are the possibilities and promises contained in the Scriptures. It is the privilege of every one of us to perfect Christian character. We are not left to grope in darkness as to how we may attain to Christian perfection, but we are assured that victory is ours if we meet the conditions for success. We ought to be encouraged by the practical examples of men and women who were victorious over sin and Satan.

Hebrews 11 gives us a record of mighty men and women of old who withstood the tide of evil that engulfed the world and were so endowed with power from on high that Satan could not stand before them.

One of the key ingredients that men and women had in Bible times was faith. They believed God and His Word and trusted in Him. Their lives were sanctified. This aroused anger in Satan and he declared war against them. They did not cower in fear of the devil, but they were courageous, full of faith, and determined.

> "Who through faith subdued kingdoms, wrought righteousness, obtained promises, stopped the mouths of lions, Quenched the violence of fire, escaped the edge of the sword, out of weakness were made strong, waxed valiant in fight, turned to flight the armies of the aliens. Women received their dead raised to life again: and others were tortured, not accepting deliverance; that they might obtain a better resurrection: And others had trial of cruel mockings and scourgings, yea, moreover of bonds and imprisonment: They were stoned, they were sawn asunder, were tempted, were slain with the sword: they wandered about in sheepskins and goatskins; being destitute, afflicted, tormented; (Of whom the world was not worthy:) they wandered in deserts, and in mountains, and in dens and caves of the earth." Hebrews 11:33-38.

The above verses tell us about the faith that the men and women of old had in God and how this led some of them to suffer pain, death, and persecution. Others were used miraculously by God to overcome tremendous odds and defeat the enemies of God.

Thanks be to God that we are not left alone. If God had abandoned us when man first sinned in the garden, we would have been left to the devil who is a merciless task master. But since God had devised a plan whereby we can be saved from the penalty and power of sin, we as humans have been engaged in constant warfare with the prince of darkness and his host of evil. We are safe only as we are surrendered to Christ. If we are not surrendered to Him, we are exposed to the enemy and become open targets. If we are not decidedly on the side of Christ we are on the side of the enemy.

The path that Jesus commands us to travel may be fraught with danger on every side, but we have the assurance that Christ will never leave us nor forsake us. The life of surrender that we are invited to endure is the way to eternal life. Any other way brings eternal death. **"There is a way that seemeth right unto a man, but the end thereof are the ways of death." Proverbs 16:25.**

We have a tremendous record of men and women of faith, and this should give us encouragement and influence us to put away sin from us.

> "Wherefore seeing we also are compassed about with so great a cloud of witnesses, let us lay aside every weight, and the sin which doth so easily beset us, and let us run with patience the race that is set before us, Looking unto Jesus the author and finisher of our faith; who for the joy that was set before him endured the cross, despising the shame, and is set down at the right hand of the throne of God." Hebrews 12:1-2.

Since we have the example of men and women of faith all over the Bible, we are to lay aside every obstacle that is keeping us from perfecting Christian character. We are to also lay aside every sin that easily entangle us. The text mentions laying aside the sin that so easily ensnare and trap us. The Lord is saying that when temptation is not met with much resistance when we encounter it, we easily give in to it. If we would just accept the power that Jesus freely offers us, we would be victorious in the struggle against temptation. We are told to "fight the good fight of faith." 1 Timothy 6:12. There is only one source that we can look to that will supply the power that we need. We are told to look unto Jesus who is "the author and finisher of our faith." Hebrews 12:2. Jesus is the source of faith. We must have the faith of Jesus if we are going to be overcomers.

The characteristics of those who are victors over the beast power is identified in Revelation 14:12. "Here is the patience of the saints: here are they that keep the commandments of God, and the faith of Jesus." Let us look at these three characteristics:

**1. Patience**

"But the fruit of the Spirit is love, joy, peace, longsuffering, gentleness, goodness, faith, meekness, temperance: against such there is no law." Galatians. 5:22, 23. One of the characteristics of those who are **not** practicing willful sin is that they are long-suffering or patient. It is one of the fruits of the Spirit. Without patience we can never endure the life of sanctification. We are tried that we may get rid of everything that is not like the character of Christ.

> "And beside this, giving all diligence, add to your faith virtue; and to virtue knowledge; And to knowledge temperance; and to temperance patience; and to patience godliness; And to godliness brotherly kindness; and to brotherly kindness charity." 2 Peter 1:5-7.

We are here given the characteristics of those who are born-again and saved by the grace of God. Right in the middle of the eight rungs of this ladder of sanctification we find patience. We are to calmly submit to God so Christ can live out His perfect life of holiness in us. We are not to murmur and complain like the children of Israel in the wilderness. "In your patience possess ye your souls." Luke 21:19. When we have patience, we are demonstrating the character of Jesus who never uttered an impatient word and He was not irritated by anyone. Long lines do not irritate and agitate us; traffic jams are a breeze; angry words do not move us; we will not murmur and complain about how rough our week was; we will not be quick to always answer someone with unkind words. Our calm and gentle demeanor will show that we have the trait of patience which is so lacking in our world today.

**2. Obedience or Commandment Keeping**

"If ye love me, keep my commandments." John 14:15. "Ye are my friends, if ye do whatsoever I command you." John 15:14. When we love Jesus, we will be obedient to Him and keep His commandments; all ten of them. Since Jesus bore our sins and credits to us His perfectly sinless life, we are to express our love and appreciation by being obedient. If we want to be the friends of Jesus, we must look like Him in character, and His commands are a reflection of His righteous character. Therefore, we are going to do His commands. Keeping the commandments of God is not a burden, but it is a privilege and protection. Commandment keeping is the natural result of a life that has been surrendered to God. It is Jesus that lives out His perfect life of righteousness in him. Obedience to the commandments is a delight.

**3. Faith**

"But without faith it is impossible to please him: for he that cometh to God must believe that he is, and that he is a rewarder of them that diligently seek him." Hebrews 11:6. **"The just shall live by faith." Romans 1:17.** We cannot please God without faith, and we can only live the sanctified life by faith.

Sanctification is God's chosen method of ridding our lives of this disease called sin. Rebellion originated in heaven and the ones who refused to repent of their sins were expelled and cast out of heaven. If we desire to take their places and go to heaven to be among holy beings, and be in the presence of the Father and Jesus His Son, we are to be sanctified here in this life. Perfection of character is not given to us at the second coming of Christ, but it is to be developed in us during our lifetime. If it is given to us at the second coming of Christ, then we would not need to have victory over sin now. We could wait until Jesus comes. But this is not the case. **"To day if ye will hear his voice, harden not your hearts." Hebrews 4:7.** This text did not say next week or when Jesus comes the second time. It says today. Postponing sanctification for a future time can be fatal. We are to be fitted for eternal life through the process of justification and sanctification today. Tomorrow is not guaranteed.

# Chapter Seventeen

# The Possibilities of Perfection-Part II

We are promised the power that is available to us to maintain a life of perfection or a life that is continually sanctified by Christ. The perfection of Christian character is possible now. If it were not so, God would not have commanded us to be holy. There can be no crown of eternal life awaiting us when Jesus comes to take us home if we do not have a perfect Christian character here on earth. The Scriptures give us hope that perfection is possible and attainable. It is within the reach of all and is not something that is so out of our reach that all we can do is to hopelessly desire it without any possibility of obtaining it. The promises in the Word are there for us to be motivated to attain to perfection of character. If Christian maturity or perfection were not possible, Christ would not have commanded us to be perfect as our heavenly Father is. We are given the command because it is possible. It is possible to overcome every know sin in our lives. It is possible to live a life of sinlessness, meaning, that it is possible to live a life that is free of every known sin. It is possible to live a life of purity, integrity, and obedience.

One of the most powerful texts in all the Bible that tells us about the assurance of perfection is found in Jude 1:24. It reads, **"Now unto him that is able to keep you from falling, and to present you faultless before the presence of his glory with exceeding joy."** This is the antidote. Jesus is the solution to the struggles that many of us encounter in our quest for the perfection of character. It is not inherent in ourselves to save ourselves. It is Christ that must do the work in us. The text says that Christ is able to keep us from falling. Is it saying that the perfection of character is possible? It surely is. It is within our grasp. If we allow Christ to reign on the throne of our hearts, we are perfect because His righteous character is in us. He does the work.

But how is it that Christ is enabled to keep us from falling? How is it that we overcome temptation? How is it that we perfect Christian character? It is only when there is a complete surrender of the will to God that we are able to live the life of perfection. Without the surrender of the will, we are entangled in sin and drawn away by our own lusts and enticed into sinning. When we surrender ourselves to Christ, His will takes possession of the citadel of our minds and He works His will in us. Christ has the ability to keep us living lives of obedience to Him. Only when we cooperate with God are we thus enabled to live sinless lives. As long as Christ is enthroned within, we do not practice willful sin. This is the assurance that we have.

There is a text of Scripture that, to some, have more questions than answers. It is found in 1 John 3:9. It says "Whosoever is born of God doth not commit sin; for his seed remaineth in him: and he cannot sin, because he is born of God." The person who is born of God does not commit willful sin and he cannot sin. Yes, you read it right. This text is not, however, talking about absolute sinlessness because someone who has experienced the new birth is not beyond the possibility of sinning because his nature is still sinful. He does not commit willful sin because Christ, who is the seed of the woman in Genesis 3:15, is in him. This text really means that the born-again saint does not practice premeditated/willful sin. It is possible that someone who has experienced the new birth in Christ to make a mistake and commit sin but this does not mean that sinning is his habitual practice. He slipped up, made a mistake, and sinned. The direction in which this man is going is not downward, but upward. The habits tend toward heaven, and not hell.

If a person who is born again willfully sins against God, it means that he severed the connection he had with God so that he could sin. He broke off the relationship (connection) he had enjoyed with God and followed the suggestion of Satan. The soul must consent to sin and purposefully let go of the hand of God in order to willfully sin. The soul cannot and will not sin willfully if Christ is enthroned within. It is when Christ is not enthroned within that a person sins willfully. You may be wondering why so much is said to explain the meaning of 1 John 3:9, but this is done so that no one will doubt the true meaning of that text. No one should come away believing that because they made a mistake and sinned that there is no hope. However, no one should get the idea that he can willfully sin and simultaneously continue to have an unbroken connection with God. If a person willfully sins against God, that person must make haste, repent, and forsake their sin.

God is willing and ready to forgive, because we read that "If we confess our sins, he is faithful and just to forgive us our sins, and to cleanse us from all unrighteousness." 1 John 1:9.

The person who is born of God does not experience an "up-and-down" relationship with Christ where he sins today and he is in Christ tomorrow, and then he sins the next day, and is in Christ the following day. This is not victory over sin. This is not being born again. The born-again believer must be brought to the point where he is experiencing an unbroken relationship with Christ. However, there may be rare occasions where he falls into a temptation and sins against God, but this drives him to his knees in confession and repentance. He is broken and contrite, and the thought that He has hurt the heart of His Saviour fills him with pain and he forsakes the sin. Falling into willful sin does not habitually, and frequently happen to the one who is born of God. The key is, he does not practice willful sin or sin is not a regular habit of his. **Note: A person who was in Christ but falls into sin and strays away to the point where he is lost must not lose hope. There is mercy with God. However, that person must not think that time is on his side. He is to make haste and hurry back into the arms or Jesus where there is grace, mercy, protection, and a life of peace, rest, and happiness.**

There is a difference between the one who is born of God and makes a mistake, and the one who cares not about whether he sins. The one who is born of God does not believe that he can go on doing wrong and just ask for forgiveness each time and keeps on sinning repeatedly. The one who constantly sins against God with impunity and regularly practices sin is not born of God because he does not experience victory over willful sin. To believe that it is ok to sin and just ask for forgiveness is not a belief or doctrine found in the Scriptures. We are taught to repent and forsake our sins. When sin is abandoned, the believer is born of God.

There was a man who was afraid of being seen in public talking to Jesus, so he decided to seek an interview with Jesus at night. His name was Nicodemus. He acknowledged Jesus as only a teacher sent from God when he met with Him that night, but Jesus did not waste any time in rebuking Him for not recognizing who He really was. Jesus was about to reveal to him some of the most precious promises that are found in all the Bible.

The first thing Jesus said to him was this: "Except a man be born again, he cannot see the kingdom of God." John 3:3. This statement was true for Nicodemus and it is the requirement for entrance into the kingdom of God. This is what must happen to the child of God if the kingdom of heaven will be set up in the throne of his heart (mind). There are no ifs, ands, and buts about this matter. This is the only condition because being born again means that a person has been convicted of sin, he has confessed them, he has repented of them, he has accepted the sacrifice of Christ as the means of deliverance from the penalty of sin. Being born again also means the child of God has accepted the perfectly righteous life of Christ as the means of becoming justified in the sight of God and he is now living the sanctified life. He is now in the realm of sanctification or in the stage where he is perfect, meaning that he is not willfully sinning against God.

The phrase, "born again," is also another term for the "new birth experience." It is also referred to as "conversion." When a sinner becomes born again, he has passed from eternal death into eternal life because his sins are pardoned and he has made a choice to be a member of the family of God. A public declaration of his transformation from a life of sin to a life of righteousness and obedience is demonstrated by the act of baptism. The symbol of baptism is not the reality but it is just what it is, a symbol. It cannot take the place of the new birth experience but is a command given to us, and everyone who joins the family of God is required to publicly get baptized.

If the conditions for receiving the new birth experience are met, then that person is a candidate for baptism. It is a sad fact that there are hundreds of thousands and even millions of people who have become members of the churches of today through the rite of baptism and were not truly born again and converted. They accepted and agreed to some of the doctrines that are in the Bible and were passed off as being qualified for baptism. These have not experienced true conversion although they are in the church, but have no real sustaining connection with Christ. They try to supply the lack of a vitalizing relationship of obedience and faith in Jesus with various things. They try to work up their emotions by getting their minds into a spiritual high through praise and worship in the church. They use this to substitute the emptiness they have inside their hearts and think that the high they experience in worship and praise is what constitutes their relationship with Christ.

The born-again believer does not use man-made substitutes to satisfy his inner longings after God. The Bible is very clear in outlining the steps to Christ. Any other method of working up a relationship with Christ is satanic and unbiblical. Satan is a master deceiver and invents ways to trap us and make us believe that we are in Christ when we are really not in Christ. We are to search the Scriptures thoroughly so that we can identify the snares of Satan.

Unless we do this, we shall fall prey to his traps. We "shall stumble, and fall, and be broken, and be snared, and be taken." Isaiah 8:15.

The enemy is constantly watching to see whether anyone will repent and forsake his sins. When he sees that a person desires to be converted, he is aroused to action and tries to place obstacles in his way so that he stumbles and falls. One of the chief weapons he uses to cause the fall of a person who is convicted of sin and wants to be converted is the agency of the teachers and preachers of the gospel. The teachers and preachers of the gospel calm the concerns of a conscientious soul by telling that person that all he must do is to believe. In other words, all he must do is to have a mental ascent to the part of the gospel where Jesus died for his sins. If he believes that Jesus died for his sins and accepts Jesus as his personal Saviour then that is enough. The part where Jesus becomes Lord of his life is omitted and is basically a suggestion to them. To these false teachers and deceived ministers, the law of God was nailed to the cross and they do not have to abide by a set of rules. They claim to be free in Jesus.

These men have been deceived into thinking that obedience to the law of God is not a doctrine or teaching in the Bible. They claim that the blood of Jesus covers them and they are released from the "bondage" of keeping the law. They try to silence the voice of conscience by crowding their lives with everything but what they need. They are spiritually poor, blind, and naked. They are also wretched and miserable. This condition too accurately describes the majority, of not just ministers and teachers, but the majority of those who claim to be Christians in the world today.

The solution to the problem of those who have the above conditions of spiritual poverty, blindness, nakedness, and a life filled with wretchedness and misery is found in the offer that our Saviour so lovingly and mercifully makes.

> "Come unto me, all ye that labour and are heavy laden, and I will give you rest. Take my yoke upon you, and learn of me; for I am meek and lowly in heart: and ye shall find rest unto your souls. For my yoke is easy, and my burden is light." Matthew 11:28-30.

Does this sound too good to be true? It is not too good to be true, but it so good because it is true. Those who are stuck in limbo as far as their connection with God is concerned, will find, in this, the solution to their stagnant Christian journey. Those who are burdened and stressed, will find in Jesus their all in all. Those who are weighed down with the guilt of sins will find that if they come to Jesus, they will find rest unto their souls.

In the text above, Christ appeals to us to take His yoke upon us. This yoke is the same as the cross. This cross is a symbol of surrender and submission. If we humbly surrender our hearts to Christ, we will find that the things that perplex and annoy us will be held at bay and we will live the abundant life in Christ. Our lives will not be free of trials, but we will have the power to live above our trials and even our trials will turn into blessings.

Christ says that His yoke is easy and His burden is light. Is this really true? The reason why we find the Christian life so hard is that many of us have not severed the connection we have with the world and sin. Righteousness and sin cannot coexist. They are diametrically opposed to each other and cannot dwell in the heart contemporaneously. It is one or the other. Jesus said that "No man can serve two masters: for either he will hate the one, and love the other; or else he will hold to the one, and despise the other. Ye cannot serve God and mammon." Matthew 6:24. Once the world is crucified to us, and us to the world, we will find that the cross or yoke of submission is an easy matter. We will say like David, "I delight to do thy will, O my God: yea, thy law is within my heart." Psalm 40:8. Living the Christian life becomes easy after we become dead to sin. The lack of a heart or mind that is dead to sin is the reason why there are so many wretched and miserable professed Christians.

The world today is filled with many professors of Christianity. These do not know what it is to surrender to Christ and therefore they do not enjoy the abundant life that Christ offers. They shrink from the cross and have a big problem with the yoke that Christ gives. They think that it is too much to sacrifice their way of life for the sake of living the surrendered life and so they convince themselves that a life of ease is the way to eternal life. We are told that a life of ease is the road that leads to destruction.

> "Enter ye in at the strait gate: for wide is the gate, and broad is the way, that leadeth to destruction, and many there be which go in thereat: Because strait is the gate, and narrow is the way, which leadeth unto life, and few there be that find it." Matthew 7:13-14.

The gate that leads to destruction has many attractions that are near and dear to the human heart and this way leads to eternal doom, and death. The gate that leads to eternal life is narrow. There is only one way to eternal life and that is through a life of self-denial and self-abnegation. There is no room for the supposed enjoyment of a life of ease that may be found on the wide gate and the broad way. The text says that there are few who even find the strait gate. The reason why this is the case is that most people refuse the offer that Christ makes and have chosen the way that the enemy of souls offers.

I have come to realize that the attractions of this present evil world do not bring lasting peace, joy, and happiness. Their tendency is to leave us thirsting for more and we are never truly satisfied with the things this world offers. This is the nature of the things of this world. On the other hand, the things that Jesus offers us are satisfying and eternal. They will not leave us empty and unfulfilled. Even in this present world we can live the abundant life where our lives are filled with love, joy, peace, rest, and happiness. The things that we are commanded to give up are the very things that steal from us peace, joy, and happiness. When God commands us to give up anything that is harmful to us, He supplies the void with something better.

> "I have set the LORD always before me: because he is at my right hand, I shall not be moved. Therefore my heart is glad, and my glory rejoiceth: my flesh also shall rest in hope. For thou wilt not leave my soul in hell; neither wilt thou suffer thine Holy One to see

corruption. Thou wilt shew me the path of life: in thy presence is fulness of joy; at thy right hand there are pleasures for evermore." Psalm 16:8-11.

Did you see what causes our hearts to be glad? It is the result of setting the Lord always before us and the fact that He is at our right hand or beside us. When we walk with the Lord, and we allow Him to be the King of our lives, our hearts are made glad, we rejoice and we have hope. God will not abandon us to be destroyed by Satan. We experience fullness of joy in the presence of Christ. The path that He marks out for us is the way to life. He constantly provides for us pleasures forevermore. This abundant life is freely given to us. Many have not experienced this because they do not trust in God to believe that this is so. They do not believe that this kind of life is possible without embracing the things that the world offers, and so, they miss out on the blessing of a prosperous life. This is not about a prosperous life as far as money, possessions, education, and temporal prosperity are concerned, but about the abundant life that Jesus offers. True joy is not found in having temporal prosperity, but it is found in Jesus. Temporal prosperity does not give us real peace. A person may have all the advantages, riches, education, and fame in this world, but these are not the source of real joy and satisfaction. Satan peddles these as the things to chase after, but they are not the source of peace. "For unto us a child is born, unto us a son is given: and the government shall be upon his shoulder: and his name shall be called Wonderful, Counsellor, the mighty God, the everlasting Father, **the Prince of Peace.**" Isaiah 9:6.

It is true that we need money and certain things to make life more bearable, but at the end of the day it is the born-again experience that will guarantee our peace and joy in this world and the one to come. We are told that **"the way of transgressors is hard." Proverbs 13:15.** The way of the sinner leads to destruction.

> "Therefore take no thought, saying, What shall we eat? or, What shall we drink? or, Wherewithal shall we be clothed? (For after all these things do the Gentiles seek:) for your heavenly Father knoweth that ye have need of all these things." Matthew 6:31-32.

Jesus warns us not to be as the world and be so caught up in what we shall eat and what we shall wear because God knows what we are in need of. He goes on to say that the Gentiles are caught up with the thought of what to eat and what to wear. Our main concern must be to live in the light of God's presence and power and living a life of total surrender and submission to the Lord. Anything other than this is a sure way to land us on the road that leads to eternal death.

> "But seek ye first the kingdom of God, and his righteousness; and all these things shall be added unto you." Matthew 6:33.

One of the possibilities of perfection is the wonderful assurance of contentment. To be content with whatever we possess is a condition that requires us to so love the Lord, that wherever He may lead us, and in whatever state we are in, we will be satisfied, and thankful.

> "Not that I speak in respect of want: for I have learned, in whatsoever state I am, therewith to be content. I know both how to be abased, and I know how to abound: every where and in all things I am instructed both to be full and to be hungry, both to abound and to suffer need. I can do all things through Christ which strengtheneth me." Philippians 4:11-13.

These three verses of Scripture are opposed to the quest for a life of ease. They tell us that we must be satisfied with the place where God has placed us. We must be content with what we have. "He that hasteth to be rich hath an evil eye, and considereth not that poverty shall come upon him." Proverbs 28:22. If the Lord sees it fit to give us more then He will give us more. We are not to try and take matters into our own hands and chase after the things of this world. If we remain faithful to God, He will give us the things that we stand in need of.

Paul says that He has learned to be content with abundance and he has learned contentment when he suffered need. In other words, if he has abundance, he is satisfied, and if he does not have enough of what he needs, he is still satisfied. He follows up this by qualifying his statement. He says that he can do all things, or the things in the two verses before, through Christ who gives him the strength. This is the key. Christ is the One who supplies the power to live a life of contentment. This possibility is within the reach of all who come to Jesus in submission and surrender. In this same chapter of Philippians, we are given the promise that our needs will be supplied. "But my God shall supply all your need according to his riches in glory by Christ Jesus." Philippians. 4:19.

A wonderful promise is given to anyone who separates himself from the wicked and delights in obedience to God or who takes pleasure in the process of sanctification or perfection of character. Obedience to God is what we ought to delight in.

> "Blessed is the man that walketh not in the counsel of the ungodly, nor standeth in the way of sinners, nor sitteth in the seat of the scornful. But his delight is in the law of the LORD; and in his law doth he meditate day and night. And he shall be like a tree planted by the rivers of water, that bringeth forth his fruit in his season; his leaf also shall not wither; and whatsoever he doeth shall prosper." Psalm 1:1-3

Those who do not follow the wicked suggestions of the ungodly are blessed; those who do not join with sinners in the path of sin are blessed; those who are not found in the company of mockers or scorners are blessed of God. Take pleasure in the Word of God and do them. Meditate upon the Scriptures day and night. Fulfill these five conditions in verses one and two and you will be like a tree planted by the rivers of water that bear fruit in its season. You shall not fade away, but whatever you do shall prosper. Abundant blessings from God are given to those who are sanctified by the truth which is the Bible. These three verses offer us wonderful possibilities if only we will allow the truth to sanctify us.

**"Sanctify them through thy truth: thy word is truth." John 17:17.**

We are made holy by the Word of God which is the Bible because:

> "The word of God is quick, and powerful, and sharper than any twoedged sword, piercing even to the dividing asunder of soul and spirit, and of the joints and marrow, and is a discerner of the thoughts and intents of the heart." Hebrews 4:12.

The Scriptures is what sanctifies, purifies, purges, and perfects us. If we do the commandments of God, we will perfect Christian character. **We are commanded to be perfect and whenever God commands us to do something He provides the power to do it.**

The ones that God sanctifies or makes perfectly holy are called saints or holy ones. To submit to God requires the giving up of the world and the attractions and distractions that are in it.

**"Gather my saints together unto me; those that have made a covenant with me by sacrifice." Psalm 50:5.**

The saints are those that have entered into a covenant or agreement with God by sacrifice. We must lay all on the altar of sacrifice. If we really want eternal life, we will do whatever it takes to secure it. We will give Jesus our hearts (minds) so that He can perfect His character in us. The possibilities of perfection require a sacrifice of everything that is not like the character of Christ. We ought to be willing to give up everything we hold dear if necessary to secure for ourselves the hope and reality of eternal life. If we are willing to be made willing, the Holy Spirit supplies the power for us to make a complete surrender of ourselves to God regardless of the sacrifice required. The peace of God will then be our comfort and we are assured of victory over sin and a life of satisfaction and fulfilment.

Whatever it takes is the motto of every true child of God. Paul wrote to the Hebrews and said something that needs to be considered by us and applied to our very lives. **"Ye have not yet resisted unto blood, striving against sin." Hebrews 12:4.**

The fight against sin is the good fight of faith in Jesus and we must be ready to resist sin to the point where we would rather die than sin against God. **"And they overcame him by the blood of the Lamb, and by the word of their testimony; and they loved not their lives unto the death." Revelation 12:11.**

It is the death of Jesus that takes us from death to life and it is through this, along with the experience of sanctification and the perfection of character that Satan is overcome. If we do not accept the death of Jesus as the atonement for our sins along with having the experience of the new birth, we cannot defeat Satan. The sanctified life is critical if there is going to be any hope of escaping the snares of Satan.

Precious are all the promises that are contained in the Scriptures that show us the possibilities of perfection. May we be determined to allow the power of God to do the work of purification that our souls are in need of. May we never listen to the suggestion of Satan that tells us that perfection of Christian character is not necessary and is impossible. It is possible to live the victorious life; it is possible to live the sanctified life; it is possible to perfect Christian character; it is possible to live a life that pleases God. The possibilities are yours for the taking. Be wise and choose the right way which is the way to eternal life.

# Chapter Eighteen

# Ultimate Perfection

The title of this chapter may suggest doubts concerning the possibility of human beings eventually reaching the point where they are so perfect that they will not sin at all in this life. Yet this is the condition that will be reached by the group of saints who will be alive when Jesus comes. They will not die at all, but will be preserved during the time of trouble that is coming upon the world. They will fully reflect the perfectly righteous character of Christ under the most severe and trying circumstances that man has ever been called upon to endure. We will take a look at this subject and this characteristic of ultimate perfection exemplified by these saints.

The word ultimate, as an adjective, according to Google, means being or happening at the end of a process, or final. Synonyms for ultimate include "eventual, last, final, concluding, and subsequent." Google.com. As a noun, it means "the best achievable or imaginable of its kind." Google.com. Synonyms in this case include "utmost, height, peak, zenith, pinnacle." Google.com. Perfection is a state of completeness or maturity.

The character of Christ is held out to us as the great standard by which we are to judge our own characters. Jesus was fully imbued with the Holy Spirit. His character was totally perfect and He was totally surrendered to God. So perfect was His character, He could say "the prince of this world cometh, and hath nothing in me." John 14:30. Jesus was the only one that has ever been born on this earth that has never sinned and therefore He is our only perfect example. The sacrificial lamb in the Old Testament could not have any spot or blemish if it was going to be fit for sacrifice. So it was with Jesus. His character was totally and completely perfect, therefore the Father accepted Him as the One who could atone for our sins by bearing our sins on the cross. His life of total surrender and perfect righteousness was accepted by the Father and we are justified in His presence. We have the title to heaven through justification, but the Christ life must be lived out in us through sanctification which perfects our characters and gives us our fitness for heaven.

During the period where our characters are made perfect or complete, we might sin against God. The child of God who maintains that vital connection with God continually may hit a bump in the road and sin against Him. These rare sins are not the regular practice of our lives but occur as a result of various trials and tribulations that we may experience. It may very well be that there is a momentarily lapse in the relationship of total surrender where we give in to temptation and slip and sin against our Maker. We become sorry for hurting the tender heart of our God, and quickly turn away and forsake our sin. We then renew the life of surrender we had with Him before we sinned. The converted soul that sins against God does not sin against God as a practice, but slips up rarely. This is the exception and not the rule of his life.

On the other hand, there are those who know to do right but have fallen into a life of sin and have become entangled and imprisoned by sin. There is hope in Jesus. Giving up is what Satan wants and he is constantly trying to sink you deeper into the depths of sin, so much so, that you reach the point of no return, but there is no soul so deeply sunken into sin that Jesus cannot deliver. There is assurance of victory in Jesus. Your sins can be pardoned. The only sins that cannot be pardoned are the ones that have not been confessed and forsaken. The repentant soul must see his need and be broken and contrite. He sees his true condition of helplessness and runs to the One who possesses the power to free him from sin.

Note: It is possible that even at this moment you might be struggling with sin and you have not the assurance of victory over it, but you are not to give up in dismay. Trust in God and He will make you an overcomer if you let Him in. The Holy Spirit will empower you if you willingly give up control and let Him fight your battles.

The time will come when there will be a group of people on this planet that will reflect the perfect character of Jesus so fully that He will recognize this fact and come back the second time to claim them as His own. The perfect character of Christ in His people is what will precipitates His second coming. This group of saints will have complete victory over sin. They will not struggle with sin and are completely sinless. This sounds unbelievable but it is not so because the Bible tells us of this group. Read on and you will discover the truth concerning this.

We read in Matthew 24:14 that "this gospel of the kingdom shall be preached in all the world for a witness unto all nations; and then shall the end come." The gospel will be effectively preached to all the world through the witness of God's people. This witness is the perfectly righteous character of Christ exemplified by His people. When the world sees this loving and holy character of Christ reflected in His people, they will recognize the fact that "they had been with Jesus." Acts 4:13. Many who see this demonstration of love, compassion, mercy, courage, selflessness, and sinlessness in the lives of the children of God will take their stand for Jesus and will join their ranks. A part of the number of these new converts will go through the time of trouble and will not die, but will live to see Jesus's second coming. There are many who are not yet part of God's remnant church who will leave the fallen churches and make their stand with them when they see the character of Jesus fully demonstrated in the lives of His people. We all have before us, a glorious opportunity to shine as lights so the world may see Jesus in us. "Let your light so shine before men, that they may see your good works, and glorify your Father which is in heaven." Matthew 5:16.

What does the Bible have to say about the proclamation of the gospel, the time of trouble, and the end of the world?

"But in the days of the voice of the seventh angel, when he shall begin to sound, the mystery of God should be finished, as he hath declared to his servants the prophets." Revelation 10:7. The phrase "when he shall begin to sound" also means "when He is about to sound." There is a narrow window between the close of the preaching of the gospel and the second coming of Jesus. The mystery of God is the gospel or the good news of the plan of salvation and it will be preached in all the world for a witness which is the character of Christ revealed in His people."

"And for me, that utterance may be given unto me, that I may open my mouth boldly, to make known the mystery of the gospel." Ephesians 6:19. God's last final call to the world to repent from their sins will be given shortly before the time of trouble and the second coming of Christ.

We are told of a time of trouble that will come upon the earth that will be so great that it will be the greatest time of trouble that the earth would have ever experienced since the nations came into existence. This time of trouble is recorded in the book of Daniel.

> "And at that time shall Michael stand up, the great prince which standeth for the children of thy people: and there shall be a time of trouble, such as never was since there was a nation even to that same time: and at that time thy people shall be delivered, every one that shall be found written in the book. And many of them that sleep in the dust of the earth shall awake, some to everlasting life, and some to shame and everlasting contempt. And they that be wise shall shine as the brightness of the firmament; and they that turn many to righteousness as the stars for ever and ever." Daniel 12:1-3.

Daniel 12:1 is one of the most pivotal in all the Bible and starts out by saying "and at that time." What time is it talking about? We must look at the previous verse or verses to get an accurate picture of what precedes the time of trouble.

> "But tidings out of the east and out of the north shall trouble him: therefore he shall go forth with great fury to destroy, and utterly to make away many. And he shall plant the tabernacles of his palace between the seas in the glorious holy mountain; yet he shall come to his end, and none shall help him." Daniel 11:44-45.

The power identified in these two verses is called "The King of the North." When this power comes to an end, there will be such trouble on the earth that no pen can describe. This power will experience a destruction so bad that it will meet its doom and come to an end. The world will be plunged into trouble so great, that no previous time of trouble experience since the dawn of the nations will even come near to the severity, intensity, and destructive nature of this one.

Daniel 12:1-3 gives us an insight into the fate of the children of God. The first verse tells us that the people of God who go through the time of trouble will be delivered. It does not say that they are slain for the sake of the gospel; it does not say that they die at all. It says that they are delivered. So it can be a safe thing to conclude that they will not die. Immediately following the events of verse one, events associated with the second coming of Christ are thereby recorded. It mentions that some will be resurrected to everlasting life, and there will be some that are resurrected to face everlasting contempt. This latter group are none but the ones who pierced Jesus, the ones who delivered him up to be crucified, and the ones who have been the bitterest opposers of Christ and his people. "Hereafter shall ye see the Son of man sitting on the right hand of power, and coming in the clouds of heaven." Matthew 26:64. "Behold, he cometh with clouds; and every eye shall see him, and they also which pierced him: and all kindreds of the earth shall wail because of him. Even so, Amen." Revelation 1:7.

The group of people that will never die and will live to see the second coming of Christ is the very group that will experience ultimate perfection during this time of trouble. We now turn to the book of Revelation to look more closely at the character of these righteous ones.

> "And after these things I saw four angels standing on the four corners of the earth, holding the four winds of the earth, that the wind should not blow on the earth, nor on the sea, nor on any tree. And I saw another angel ascending from the east, having the seal of the living God: and he cried with a loud voice to the four angels, to whom it was given to hurt the earth and the sea, Saying, Hurt not the earth, neither the sea, nor the trees, till we have sealed the servants of our God in their foreheads. And I heard the number of them which were sealed: and there were sealed an hundred and forty and four thousand of all the tribes of the children of Israel." Revelation 7:1-4.

These verses tell us that there are four angels holding the winds of the earth, that they should not blow on the earth, nor on the sea, nor on any tree until the servants of God have been sealed in their foreheads. This hurting of the earth is the same time of trouble that is recorded in Daniel chapter 12. The four corners of the earth represent the four major points of the compass, east, west, north, and south. The four winds represent, strife, war, and political commotion. (See Daniel 7:2, and Jeremiah 25:32). The book of Daniel tells the prophecies and the book of Revelation enlarges on the prophecies. Revelation 7:4 tells us the number of those that are sealed. This is the same group of people that Daniel 12:1 says are delivered in the time of trouble. (If you are interested in an advanced study of the books of Daniel and Revelation, you are encouraged to obtain a copy of the book "Daniel and the Revelation" by Uriah Smith if you don't have one already.)

When probation for all mankind closes is when the destiny of everyone alive on the earth is finally decided and there can be no reversal of the choice each person has made, whether to receive the mark of the beast or whether to receive the seal of God. The mark of the beast will be enforced when the inhabitants of the earth will be brought to the point where they will be given an ultimatum. "And that no man might buy or sell, save he that had the mark, or the name of the beast, or the number of his name." Revelation 13:17. The powers that be, will force the world to accept their mark, and this worldwide movement will be an indication that life as we know it, or business as usual, will come to a sudden end, and Jesus comes back the second time.

There will come a time when only those who accept the mark of the beast will be able to buy or sell. You will not be able to purchase anything whatsoever without this mark. This will happen worldwide. The economy or commerce will be used to force men into submission but the true children of God will refuse this mark. There is a trend that is seen in the world of commerce today where we are drifting towards a cashless society. There are businesses that will not accept cash. If cash and coins become obsolete and we can only use credit or debit cards, or some other form of payment to buy and sell, then all the authorities have to do to shut us down, is to disable these cards or other payment methods. Do you see the handwriting on the wall? Do you see the manipulation and control tactics that will be enforced on society? Cashless transactions are becoming more and more popular. A cashless society is a way the powers that be will use to enforce their philosophies and aims on humanity, and is a tool that will be used by those who enforce the mark of the beast.

Anyone who refuses to accept the mark of the beast will be cut off from trade and buying or selling. God's people will be brought to the test, so now is the time for us to get right with God, and repent of our sins.

Those who refuse the mark of the beast are the ones who receive the seal of God. The beast has a mark and God has His own mark or seal. The seal of God is contained in the fourth commandment. A seal contains a name, a title, and a domain.

> "Remember the sabbath day, to keep it holy. Six days shalt thou labour, and do all thy work: But the seventh day is the sabbath of the LORD thy God: in it thou shalt not do any work, thou, nor thy son,

nor thy daughter, thy manservant, nor thy maidservant, nor thy cattle, nor thy stranger that is within thy gates: For in six days the LORD made heaven and earth, the sea, and all that in them is, and rested the seventh day: wherefore the LORD blessed the sabbath day, and hallowed it." Exodus 20:8-11.

The Sabbath is the seal of God. The fourth commandment contains the name of God which is the Lord. The Sabbath contains the title of God which is Creator. ("For in six days the LORD made heaven and earth, the sea, and all that in them is.") The Sabbath commandment mentions the territory or domain over which the Lord reigns or rules which is heaven and earth.

The final test that will come to man is whether He will choose the Sabbath or Sunday. This will be the deciding factor, and when all the earth has chosen a side, the end of mercy for the guilty inhabitants of the earth will come, but God's righteous people will be shielded and protected during the time of trouble. The seven last plagues will be poured out on the wicked.

The mark of the beast is Sunday because the beast power of Revelation 13 claims that their act of changing the Sabbath of Exodus 20 to Sunday is their mark of authority. (For more information see E.G. White's book "The Great Controversy" Chapter 35.) The Roman Catholic Church has a leader called the Pope and he claims to be the Vicar or representative of Christ. Catholic means universal. This church thinks that it has the right to control the minds of everyone on the planet. This is contrary to the Bible. The time will come when those who refuse to accept this false sabbath will be persecuted, imprisoned, bribed, maligned, and hunted down like wild animals. The United States will take the lead in the enforcement of Sunday observance on its citizens and the rest of world will follow in her footsteps to trample upon the rights of man.

The people of God who are alive at the close of probation or the end of mercy for this wicked earth will go through the time of trouble that will happen because most of the people on this planet will reject God's offer of love and mercy and will accept Satan's rule. This will be done through the enforcement of Sunday observance by law. During this decree, the mystery of God will be finished, meaning that the gospel will be preached to all the world and everyone will see the character of Christ demonstrated in His children. When this happens, the end will come when the final time of trouble will happen. We are fast approaching that time.

The law enforcing Sunday will be exalted above the Bible Sabbath and men will have to choose between the commandments of God and the commandments of men.

Now that we have identified the righteous group of people that will be alive to witness the second coming of Christ, let us look at their characteristics.

> "And I looked, and, lo, a Lamb stood on the mount Sion, and with him an hundred forty and four thousand, having his Father's name written in their foreheads. And I heard a voice from heaven, as the voice of many waters, and as the voice of a great thunder: and I heard the voice of harpers harping with

their harps: And they sung as it were a new song before the throne, and before the four beasts, and the elders: and no man could learn that song but the hundred and forty and four thousand, which were redeemed from the earth. These are they which were not defiled with women; for they are virgins. These are they which follow the Lamb whithersoever he goeth. These were redeemed from among men, being the firstfruits unto God and to the Lamb. And in their mouth was found no guile: for they are without fault before the throne of God." Revelation 14:1-5.

Below is a summary of the 144,000 as described in the preceding verses:

1. They stand with Christ on Mount Zion.

2. The Father's name is written in their foreheads. The Father declared his name to Moses of old. **"And the LORD descended in the cloud, and stood with him there, and proclaimed the name of the LORD. And the LORD passed by before him, and proclaimed, The LORD, The LORD God, merciful and gracious, longsuffering, and abundant in goodness and truth, Keeping mercy for thousands, forgiving iniquity and transgression and sin, and that will by no means clear the guilty." Exodus 34:5-7.**

3. They sing and play with their harps.

4. They sing a new song.

5. Only this group could sing this new song.

6. They were redeemed from the earth. Daniel 12:1 uses the phrase "thy people shall be delivered." This is the same group of saints.

7. They are the first fruits that are presented to the Father and to His Son Jesus Christ. It is only fitting because this group would have gone through the same kind of trouble and distress that Jesus went through at the closing scenes of His earthly mission. The phrase "first fruits," in this context, means the first portion or pledge of the great harvest of redeemed saints that will take place at the second coming of Christ that are presented to the Father and the Son. This is a high honor that is afforded the 144,000 or the ones that experience ultimate perfection before the second coming of Christ. The term "first fruits" can be also called a gift or offering.

8. In their mouth is found no guile. The word guile means "craftiness, deviousness, cunning, slyness." Merriam-Webster Dictionary. The 144,000 exemplify the righteous character of Christ.

9. They are without fault. The saints of God who go through the time of trouble will have characters that are so pure that all that is seen is a faultless character. The 144,000 experience ultimate perfection in the midst of the most trying circumstances that a group of human beings could have ever experienced.

As mentioned above, the 144,000 living saints have no guile in their mouth. The reason why they have no guile in their mouths is that they have been justified and fully sanctified. They have experienced complete victory over sin. They have fully attained to perfection. They have reached a point where they are beyond the power of Satan. They have reached a point where they cannot fall. All this is the characteristic of those saints who go through the time of trouble that is soon to come upon the earth. They have passed the final test of the Sunday law and have withstood the beast. They are without fault as the text mentions. They are flawless and faultless.

We are told that Jesus will present to Himself **"a glorious church, not having spot, or wrinkle, or any such thing." Ephesians 5:27.** This verse is key in proving the fact concerning the complete perfection of the people of God before Jesus comes the second time. There are some who may object to this belief but the Bible says it and I believe it and that's it. It is the truth. It sounds incredible but it is so. At this present time when we look at the condition of the church in the world it is hard to imagine that there will come a time when everyone of God's true people will be perfect. God's true church or people are not everyone who are members of the body of believers and have their names in the church books, but are the ones who live a life of total commitment to Jesus and experience victory over sin. "For many are called, but few are chosen." Matthew 22:14.

What kind of trouble will the 144,000 go through? "Alas! for that day is great, so that none is like it: it is even the time of Jacob's trouble; but he shall be saved out of it." Jeremiah 30:7. The time of trouble that those who experience ultimate perfection will go through is called "the time of Jacob's trouble. What was the experience that Jacob went through?

> "And Jacob was left alone; and there wrestled a man with him until the breaking of the day. And when he saw that he prevailed not against him, he touched the hollow of his thigh; and the hollow of Jacob's thigh

was out of joint, as he wrestled with him. And he said, Let me go, for the day breaketh. And he said, I will not let thee go, except thou bless me. And he said unto him, What is thy name? And he said, Jacob. And he said, Thy name shall be called no more Jacob, but Israel: for as a prince hast thou power with God and with men, and hast prevailed." Genesis 32:24-28.

Jacob had stolen the paternal blessing from his brother Esau and now, in his estimation, he was to suffer death at his hands. He saw no way out and decided to spend the night in prayer to God for deliverance. As he prayed, he confessed his sins and did some deep soul searching. He was determined to press his petition to God because he thought he was about to die and God was His only hope. While he was petitioning God with earnest cries and tears, a strong hand was laid upon him. His first thought was that it was an enemy that was seeking his life. He immediately began trying to escape from the grasp of his "Unknown Assailant." This wrestling continued until near the break of day. Jacob wrestled in the dark with this "mysterious Person," and he put forth all his effort to gain the mastery, but to no avail.

When "the supposed enemy" saw that He was not overpowering Jacob, He touched the hollow of Jacob's thigh and it was out of joint. When Jacob saw what was done, he realized and discerned the true nature of "the supposed enemy" he was wrestling with. He was wrestling with "Someone from heaven" and he did not know it at first. In the midst of this handicap and excruciating pain, he was even more persevering and his faith grew even stronger.

He was not about to let this moment pass by without receiving the assurance of pardon and protection from God. He said to this heavenly Messenger, "I will not let thee go, except thou bless me." The heavenly Messenger now blesses Jacob and changes his name to Israel which means overcomer.

The 144,000 who go through the time of Jacob's trouble will have a similar experience as Jacob in that they will be praying for deliverance from their enemies. They will be in agony of spirit and will engage in deep soul searching. Satan and his host of evil angels will taunt, and mock them. They will be hunted down by wicked men and will find no way out except by the mercies of God. They will wrestle with God in prayer that they might be delivered. They will recall the mercies of God. They will plead with God to bless them by delivering them from the two beast powers of Revelation 13 and the governments and citizens of the nations all over the world. The calamities that have come upon the wicked will be blamed on the 144,000.

It is at night that the stars shine. We cannot see them in the daytime but when it is night they appear in the sky. So it is with the people of God. In the dark hour of test and trial, the 144,000 will display the character of Jesus fully. Holy angels and the inhabitants of distant worlds will see a demonstration of perfection among men that they have never before seen in such numbers and all at the same time. The Father, Son, and Holy Spirit will behold a group of mortals who will fully reflect Christ's character at the end of time.

The time of Jacob's trouble that the 144,000 experience will come after the close of the probation for all that dwell on the earth. In Revelation 7 we read that there are two groups of people. The first group is the 144,000. The second group is the great multitude which no man could number.

> "After this I beheld, and, lo, a great multitude, which no man could number, of all nations, and kindreds, and people, and tongues, stood before the throne, and before the Lamb, clothed with white robes, and palms in their hands." Revelation 7:9.

The great multitude represents the faithful who died in Christ throughout the ages, from the time of Adam until the last saint that dies at the end of earth's probation, just before the seven last plaques begin to fall and when the king of the north of Daniel 11 comes to its end. This great multitude is separate and in addition to the 144,000. The 144,000 are numbered, but the great multitude could not be numbered by any man.

The 144,000 will be the last remnant of God's last day people who will resist and refuse the mark of the beast. They will be barred from buying and selling, and every earthly support will be cut off. They will not be able to use electricity and many other services. They will lose their secular jobs, and they will not be able to do any business transactions. It will be as if they do not exist in society. They will not be permitted to live freely in society because they refuse to observe Sunday. It should be noted that those who accept the mark of the beast will receive the seven last plagues which will be poured out after the vast majority of the population of this earth refuse the offer of the gospel of salvation.

During the time of trouble there will be a famine. This is no ordinary famine because we are told that this famine is not for food.

> "Behold, the days come, saith the Lord GOD, that I will send a famine in the land, not a famine of bread, nor a thirst for water, but of hearing the words of the LORD: And they shall wander from sea to sea, and from the north even to the east, they shall run to and fro to seek the word of the LORD, and shall not find it." Amos 8:11-12.

The mystery of God would have been finished and there will remain no more mercy for the guilty inhabitants of this earth. This time of trouble will come upon them because their probationary time has run out because of the rejection of God's mercy and the great wickedness throughout the earth. When the wicked see that the wrath of God is being poured out on them, they will seek to find the people of God to give them the Word of God but it will be too late. The only reason why they will search for the Word of God is because of the calamity that they are suffering. They will lament the results. They remain unrepentant. They will search all over but will not find anyone to teach them the gospel. They are like Judas who betrayed our Lord. He was sorry for the results, but he was not sorry for bringing pain and hurt to His Lord.

Satan will have full control of the minds of all who have rejected the last call of mercy in the declaration of the mystery of God which is the gospel. The winds will be let loose and there will be such a time of war and bloodshed that we do not now anticipate. As was already noted, winds represent strife, war, and political commotion. The nations of the earth will war against each other and men will have no control over their anger because they have rejected God's offer of mercy and the restraining power of the Holy Spirit would have been withdrawn from them. They have chosen Satan as their leader and he exercises full control over them. He delights in war and bloodshed so he will have a field day with man. Trouble will be seen on every hand.

Since God will pour out the seven last plagues on the earth and Satan will exercise full control over the minds of the inhabitants who have rejected the gospel, it is so much better and wiser to choose to serve God in a time when mercy still lingers. It is true that even the righteous who endure the time of trouble will experience hardships. However, these difficulties and trials they endure and outlast will be extremely severe but bearable, and coupled with God's love and mercy. The trials that the 144,000 will go through will pale in comparison to the wrath of God that He will pour out on the wicked. So, let us choose today to serve the Lord.

The time will come when the door of mercy will be forever shut and when that time comes, whatever spiritual condition a person is in will be the condition that he will remain in. Previously the door of mercy was open and the opportunity for repentance was given to the inhabitants of the earth, but now there will be no chance of repentance towards God. Only the faithful people of God will be accepted by him.

> "And he saith unto me, Seal not the sayings of the prophecy of this book: for the time is at hand. He that is unjust, let him be unjust still: and he which is filthy, let him be filthy still: and he that is righteous, let him be righteous still: and he that is holy, let him be holy still." Revelation 22:10-11.

This declaration comes when Jesus ceases His intercessory ministry in heaven and He gets ready to come back. This happens when the gospel has been fully preached in all the world for a witness. It comes when everyone has decided that they will either be on God's side or on the side Satan. When the character of the children of God is on full display for heaven, the world and the inhabitants of the universe to see, Christ will recognize this fact by this declaration. This is a solemn moment in time. There will be nothing that can be done to reverse this declaration. It is at this moment that the wicked become completely under the control of evil. The righteous become fully committed to righteousness and they cannot sin. In the verse following the declaration, Jesus says that He comes with His reward. "And, behold, I come quickly, and my reward is with me, to give every man according as his work shall be." Revelation 22:12. The righteous receives their reward of eternal life, but the unjust receives their reward of eternal death.

God will have a people who will fully reflect His image perfectly and we are fast approaching that day. Let us get ready, stay ready, and get others ready for God's forbearance will soon come to an end.

# Chapter Nineteen

# Beyond Ultimate Perfection

The time is fast approaching when this world will come to a sudden end. Jesus will come in the clouds of heaven to rescue the 144,000 or the perfect saints who will be alive when He comes to this earth. The living saints will be delivered as was discussed in the previous chapter. The time beyond the ultimate perfection of the living saints is the time of their glorification at Christ's second coming. The dead in Christ will be resurrected and taken to heaven along with the 144,000.

> "For our conversation is in heaven; from whence also we look for the Saviour, the Lord Jesus Christ: Who shall change our vile body, that it may be fashioned like unto his glorious body, according to the working whereby he is able even to subdue all things unto himself." Philippians 3:20-21.

We are promised that when Jesus comes our bodies will be like His. We will be given glorious bodies.

We are given many more precious promises concerning what will happen when Jesus comes the second time.

> "Let not your heart be troubled: ye believe in God, believe also in me. In my Father's house are many mansions: if it were not so, I would have told you. I go to prepare a place for you. And if I go and prepare a place for you, I will come again, and receive you unto myself; that where I am, there ye may be also." John 14:1-3.

Jesus has promised that He will come back again to take us to the place that He went to prepare for us in heaven. We all, who are the people of God, have this hope that burns inside our hearts. It is hope in the coming of our Lord and Saviour, Jesus Christ. What a glorious day that will be when we see Jesus face to face.

> "Behold, I shew you a mystery; We shall not all sleep, but we shall all be changed, In a moment, in the twinkling of an eye, at the last trump: for the trumpet shall sound, and the dead shall be raised incorruptible, and we shall be changed. For this corruptible must put on incorruption, and this mortal must put on immortality. So when this corruptible shall have put on incorruption, and this mortal shall have put on immortality, then shall be brought to pass the say-

ing that is written, Death is swallowed up in victory. O death, where is thy sting? O grave, where is thy victory?" 1 Corinthians 15:51-55.

God's people who have died will not remain dead forever because there is coming a time when all that are in the graves shall hear the voice of the Son of God and the righteous will be changed from corruptible to incorruptible and from mortal to immortality. Aren't you glad for this promise? To think that we will again see our faithful loved ones who died before us if we remain faithful, ought to fill us with hope and aspiration. Death will forever be swallowed up in victory. This is good news. This is relief from misery, pain, and suffering. We have something great to look for at the end of the world. If we remain faithful to God and die before Jesus comes again, we will be given the gift of immortality. Our bodies which are prone to decay will no longer deteriorate. We will live forever in the balm of youth. There won't be any more wrinkles, gray hairs, nor memory loss. We will live in perfect health and our strength will never fail.

> "For if we believe that Jesus died and rose again, even so them also which sleep in Jesus will God bring with him. For this we say unto you by the word of the Lord, that we which are alive and remain unto the coming of the Lord shall not prevent them which are asleep. For the Lord himself shall descend from heaven with a shout, with the voice of the archangel, and with the trump of God: and the dead in Christ

shall rise first: Then we which are alive and remain shall be caught up together with them in the clouds, to meet the Lord in the air: and so shall we ever be with the Lord. Wherefore comfort one another with these words." 1 Thessalonians 4:14-18.

This passage of Scripture is one of the most exciting and expectant in all the Bible. It tells us exactly what will take place when Jesus comes the second time. There is hope beyond death. Just as how Christ was raised from the dead, even so will the righteous dead be raised from the dead. The living saints will not meet Jesus ahead of the dead in Christ who are raised.

None other than Jesus Himself, accompanied by the angelic host, will come down from heaven. He will descend with a shout. There will be no secret rapture because He will come with an audible voice. The trump of God will sound. Nothing secret about that. The dead in Christ will rise in this resurrection which is called the first resurrection or the resurrection of the righteous.

The living saints along with the newly resurrected saints, will defy the laws of gravity, and will be caught up in the clouds to meet the Lord in the air. From this point on we will forever be with Jesus. My soul is overjoyed that such a thing will be. Thank you Father, that you have not abandoned us, but you have given us the promise of life eternal and we will live forever when Jesus comes the second time. What a day of celebration and rejoicing that will be when we shall enter in through the gates into heaven.

We are told to comfort each other with the promise of deliverance when Jesus comes the second time. Let us lift up the trumpet, and let us let it ring aloud, far and near, that Jesus is coming again. I repeat, Jesus is coming again. He, the Lamb that was slain, will come again and receive us unto Himself that where He is there we may be also. He will not be coming the second time as a Lamb to the slaughter but He will come as the King of Kings and the Lord of Lords.

Daniel caught a vision of the second coming and he saw the time when **"the saints of the most High shall take the kingdom, and possess the kingdom for ever, even for ever and ever." Daniel 7:18.**

Enoch foretold of this great event and said:

> "Behold, the Lord cometh with ten thousands of his saints, To execute judgment upon all, and to convince all that are ungodly among them of all their ungodly deeds which they have ungodly committed, and of all their hard speeches which ungodly sinners have spoken against him." Jude 14-15.

John, the seer on Patmos saw it all and said:

> "And the heaven departed as a scroll when it is rolled together; and every mountain and island were moved out of their places. And the kings of the earth, and the great men, and the rich men, and the chief captains, and the mighty men, and every bondman, and every free man, hid themselves in the dens and in the rocks of the mountains; And said to the mountains and

> rocks, Fall on us, and hide us from the face of him that sitteth on the throne, and from the wrath of the Lamb: For the great day of his wrath is come; and who shall be able to stand?" Revelation 6:14-17.

The event that will be, to the righteous, one of deliverance, expectation, and joy, will be a day of wrath to the wicked. They will appeal to inanimate nature for protection against the awesome power and glory of God and of Christ. They will beg for the mountains and rocks to fall on them because, when they had the opportunity, they rejected God's offer of pardon, and spurned the appeals of the Holy Spirit. Now they have no protection against the glory of God and are slain by the brightness of Christ's second coming. They recognize that the second coming is a day of vengeance and ask the question, "who shall be able to stand?" The answer comes echoing down through the Scriptures "He that hath clean hands, and a pure heart; who hath not lifted up his soul unto vanity, nor sworn deceitfully." Psalm 24:4.

The devil does not wish for anyone to believe in the possibilities of perfection or sanctification. He wants to deprive us of the glories of the kingdom which Christ has prepared for us. He is trying to prevent us from enjoying to company of holy angels, and the inhabitants of other worlds. Satan does not want us to enjoy the companionship of God the Father, His Son Jesus, and the Holy Spirit. We will forever bask in the sunshine of the presence of Christ. Our joys and pleasures will know no end and their will be no guilty pleasure to torture our souls. Everything will be perfectly holy and there will be no death. **"But as it is written, Eye hath** not seen, nor ear heard, neither have entered into the heart of man, the thing which God hath prepared for them that love him." 1 Corinthians 2:9.** Let us not listen to the suggestions of the enemy, but let us believe and trust in God to do in us what He has promised. The Lord, who begins the good work in us will complete it.

**Perfection of Christian character is possible. It is attainable. It is not just a requirement for entry into heaven, but it is a privilege, and honor.**

Dear Lord, whatever it takes for me to be saved in the kingdom of your dear Son Jesus, do it. I lay my whole being on the altar of sacrifice for you to work in me both to will and to do of your good pleasure. Thank you, Lord, for your grace. Thank you for your mercy. Thank you for your goodness, in Jesus' name, AMEN.

www.ingramcontent.com/pod-product-compliance
Lightning Source LLC
Chambersburg PA
CBHW070548010526
44118CB00012B/1262